Digital Scrapbooking

Digital Scrapbooking

Using Your Computer to Create Exciting Scrapbook Pages

Maria Given Nerius

LARK BOOKS

A Division of Sterling Publishing Co., Inc.
New York

Editor: Jane LaFerla
Art Director: Celia Naranjo
Photographer: Steve Mann
Cover Designer: Barbara Zaretsky
Associate Art Director: Shannon Yokeley
Editorial Assistance: Delores Gosnell

Library of Congress Cataloging-in-Publication Data

Nerius, Maria.
    Digital scrapbooking : using your computer to create
exciting scrapbook pages / by Maria Given Nerius.—
1st ed.
        p. cm.
    Includes index.
    ISBN 1-57990-499-8 (hard cover)
    1. Photographs—Conservation and restoration—Data
processing. 2. Photography—Digital techniques. 3.
Photograph albums—Data processing. 4. Scrapbooks—
Data processing. 5. Digital preservation. I. Title.
TR465.N47 2004
745.593—dc22
                                        2003022185

10 9 8 7 6 5 4 3 2 1

First Edition

Published by Lark Books, a Division of
Sterling Publishing Co., Inc.
387 Park Avenue South, New York, N.Y. 10016

© 2004, Maria Nerius

Distributed in Canada by Sterling Publishing,
c/o Canadian Manda Group,
One Atlantic Ave., Suite 105
Toronto, Ontario, Canada M6K 3E7

Distributed in the U.K. by Guild of Master Craftsman
Publications Ltd., Castle Place, 166 High Street, Lewes,
East Sussex, England, BN7 1XU
Tel: (+ 44) 1273 477374, Fax: (+ 44) 1273 478606,
Email: pubs@thegmcgroup.com,
Web: www.gmcpublications.com

Distributed in Australia
by Capricorn Link (Australia) Pty Ltd.,
P.O. Box 704, Windsor, NSW 2756 Australia

If you have questions or comments about this book,
please contact:
Lark Books
67 Broadway
Asheville, NC 28801
(828) 253-0467

Manufactured in China

ISBN 1-57990-499-8

Contents

Dedication

This book is dedicated to my husband, Ken Nerius. He has always given me unconditional love and support, often having more faith in me than I do. It is only in this kind of environment that a creative person can truly grow and bloom. The only time I'm at a loss for words is when I try to thank you for making all my dreams come true.

Introduction

ONE OF MY GREATEST PLEASURES IS CREATING digital scrapbooks, then sharing that love of computer scrapbooking with my family and friends by way of the Internet. The main reason I sat down to write this book was to show you that the creativity inside of you can come out when you use your computer. There's no reason to be intimidated by digital technology when it comes to making unique and artistic scrapbook pages.

By using your photo-editing and word-processing programs in combination with your scanner and printer, you'll see how easy it is to create digital elements for decorative papers, artistic titles, and journaling. You'll learn about changing the size, color, depth, and texture of a photograph, all while sitting comfortably at your computer. Next, you'll learn how to use these elements to create pages by combining digital techniques with your traditional scrapbooking skills.

And finally, you'll learn how to create all-digital scrapbooks, slide shows, Web homepages, and Internet mail lists. My hope is that you'll discover, as I did, that using your computer in these ways opens a new dimension of fun and creativity to your work, and that you'll fall in love with digital

scrapbooking just like you fell in love with traditional scrapbooking.

I wasn't always so enthusiastic about computers. It took my husband years to convince me that using a computer could make my work as a writer easier. Once he demonstrated that using a word processing program meant I'd never have to brush out endless typos, or use carbon paper ever again, I was hooked. Today, as a professional craft writer, designer, and teacher, I work and play on my fourth generation of computer that my husband built.

I began to combine computers with scrapbooking in the early 1990s when an editor called to see if I was interested in designing scrapbook pages for publication. For inspiration, I got out the scrapbooks I made in my high school and college days—the ones I had filled with memorabilia, photos, and my illegible handwriting—only to find that most were falling apart. What a mess! I completed my assignment, then went on to restore my old scrapbooks. This time, I used my computer.

I found that by combining my knowledge of computers with traditional scrapbook skills, I got the job done faster. I also found myself charmed once again by the emotion and joy of being artistic with family and life memories. Today, I love every minute I spend scrapbooking on my computer.

HOW TO USE THIS BOOK

There are several ways to use this book. You can read it cover to cover and then start creating your own digital elements and scrapbooks. Or, if you are impatient like me, you may want to just jump in, pick a project, and refer back to the pages that explain how to work with the digital components you need. It's up to you. Most of all, have fun exploring the possibilities. Once

you master a skill, you can apply it in almost infinite ways.

In the first chapter, I talk about the elements that traditional and digital scrapbooking share. The second chapter describes how the computer's hardware, memory, and software relate to making the digital elements for your pages. If you're already accomplished on the computer, you may want to use this chapter as a review. The rest of the book is dedicated to learning digital techniques for scrapbooking. At the end of each section you will find projects that you can make or use as inspiration for creating your own pages.

When it comes to equipment, you don't need to have every, new-and-improved gadget or upgrade. Use the technology you have for now, then simply add more to your system when you feel it's time. Since many photo-editing and word-processing programs share the same features, you can apply the techniques in this book using the software you already have. And, there's no need to worry that your creations won't be archival—today's computer products are produced with long life in mind.

Are you ready to be amazed at how quickly you can create scrapbook pages and share your memories with family and friends? Let's get scrapping!

CHAPTER 1

Combining Digital Elements with Traditional Scrapbooking

It's reasonable that you might have questions when it comes to using your computer to help you create scrapbook pages. Once you understand that you don't have to abandon all the wonderful traditional scrapbooking skills, supplies, and tools you love, you'll see that the computer is just another way you can preserve your precious memories.

SCRAPBOOKING IN A DIGITAL AGE

BUT IS IT *REALLY* SCRAPBOOKING?

Many scrapbookers hesitate to use digital elements because it feels a little like cheating. Scrapbooking is supposed to be personal and hand-crafted; some people don't see the computer and its systems lending warmth and emotion to this art genre. Somehow we thought the computer would destroy the human touch valued in designing scrapbook pages.

But don't let that cold metal fool you! A computer can be used to create vibrant, heart-touching scrap-

book pages and scrapbooking embellishments. After all, since you are the one inputting data, such as photos, creative borders, and journaling, your unique personality will be reflected in your pages whether you cut and paste with scissors and glue or with the point and click of a mouse.

IS IT SAFE?

Many scrapbookers are worried about the safety of entrusting their scrapbook pages to the computer. They think that digital elements will not be archival due to the untested quality of computer paper and printer cartridge ink. However, as interest in digital scrapbooking increased, the computer industry started going out of its way to dispel these worries.

Acid-free computer paper is available at most computer stores, and don't forget that all those great acid-free scrapbooking papers you see in craft and scrapbooking stores can be used in any printer. Most printer inks have a long life if cared for properly, and you can find art sprays that will add to the paper's life. As with any scrapbook pages, you should keep them out of direct sunlight, store them in low humidity, avoid exposing them to extremes in temperature, and handle them with clean hands only.

You can safely store all of your digital elements in files and folders in your computer that you can access for years to come, rather than having them scattered around your scrapbooking area. And, by scanning all your completed scrapbook pages, you will have them at hand to quickly review for inspiration.

Moreover, if you copy and store your scrapbook pages, photographs, documents, and memorabilia on digital media like a compact disk, they have an estimated shelf life of 100 years. Like most computer technology, this is likely to be upgraded and extended within the next five to 10 years. For comparison, knowing that a video tape's lifespan is 10 years should further motivate you to begin using digital technology in your scrapbooking.

WHY SHOULD I TRY IT?

Once you feel comfortable knowing digital elements can safely be added to your treasured scrapbooking pages, you might start wondering why you should even bother adding digital elements to your scrapbooking efforts. Up until now you've been doing fine without it.

The best reason is that you can expand and explore your creativity using some of the most powerful and productive artistic tools available to you. You don't need any special skills or talents to use a computer to create dynamic scrapbook pages.

CONSIDER THE POSSIBILITES

You may need to read a few instructions or a manual, but the computer, software, scanners, printers, and digital cameras offer you almost unlimited ability to stretch your creative talents. It's not just artistic reasons that should have you excited about using your computer to scrapbook. You can save yourself time and work more efficiently. Let's take a closer look.

CONVENIENCE

One of the most important benefits of using your computer and other digital gadgets is the convenience of doing much of your work at home. This is especially important when working with photographs. You can copy or print your own photographs rather than driving to your photo developer. With photo-editing software, you can enhance your photos by adjusting the brightness, contrast, and color rather than crossing your fingers and hoping the photo technician has the time to make all those adjustments.

Think a bigger photograph would be better for your scrapbook page design? Or maybe you need to make a photo smaller? Photo-editing software makes it easy to resize photos quickly. You can even create your own contact sheets or print out wallet-size photos for a small scrapbook. You can crop a photo on your computer without cutting it by simply using a digital cropping tool found in photo software programs. You can also remove bothersome red eye and pet eye.

ARTISTIC POSSIBILITIES

You can have the pleasure of creating your own decorative background papers, instead of spending hours at a craft store or scrapbooking shop trying to find a decorative paper that will do justice to your photograph. You can create a theme for a scrapbook with a click of a mouse rather than trying to find the right sticker, die cut, paper punch, rubber stamp, or buying duplicates.

By using specialty papers in your printer, like silk, twill, poplin, or denim fabric (with paper backing so it flows smoothly through the printer), oil canvas (textured just like painting canvas), bright white, glossy, and matte, you can expand the range of looks for photos, frames, and borders. And if you get brave or just plain crafty, you can try a magnetic sheet to create refrigerator magnets, a fabric-transfer sheet to create a T-shirt, a shrink-plastic sheet to create jewelry, or window-cling sheets to share your photos with the world that walks by your front window.

Although some personal handwriting should be included in a scrapbook, there is no reason not to take advantage of the availability of attractive fonts and specialty types. Think of it—no more lightly tracing straight lines onto your scrapbook page with your pencil, while hoping you can erase those lines when you are done journaling. There is even software that allows you to turn your own handwriting into a font! You can spend more time choosing your words rather than worrying if your grandchild will be able to read your writing.

WORKING IN MULTIPLES

Using your computer to duplicate a scrapbook page or an entire scrapbook can save you time, effort, and money. All you need to do is create the page, scan it, and then print the scanned page onto quality paper. This is great for pages you design around family gatherings such as a birthday party, wedding, or family reunion. You can create several traditional scrapbook pages and print out duplicates that you place into simple binders and give as keepsakes to family and friends. Imagine how much time and effort that saves you—time you can spend creating more scrapbook pages.

MOVING TOWARD ALL-DIGITAL PAGES

Totally digital scrapbooking is addictive once you understand how easy it can be to create on your computer. There's no need to stop working on traditional scrapbooking, but don't overlook the incredible features that digital puts at your fingertips.

You can create totally digital scrapbook pages that you can send via e-mail. Or, you can create an entire digital scrapbook that you can put on CDs to mail to family and friends. You can also create a "slide show" of your scrapbook pages or favorite photos.

One of the most exciting aspects of totally digital scrapbooking and digital slide shows is that you can easily add a very special element—sound. Imagine listening to island music as you watch a slide show of a family vacation to St. Thomas, or a lively polka as you view your scrapbook of your trip to Germany.

You can also add motion! Most digital cameras have a mini-movie feature that allows you to capture 15 to 30 seconds of motion. Get out your director's cap and make your family the stars of their own scrapbooking movie. You can also transfer regular video movies onto CDs or DVDs for longer archival life and to share with others. You can design a web home page that features all your best scrapbooking pages, or create an electronic mail list to network with family, friends, or other scrapbookers around the world.

COMMON BONDS— PHOTOGRAPHY AND DESIGN BASICS

Are you inspired to create on your computer yet? Creating digitally doesn't mean you can sit back and let the computer do all the work. You need to know the principles of photography and design before you meet the monitor face to face. Taking the best photographs you can and applying proven design theories will help you create pages that please your eye. The following information will help you save time by avoiding common mistakes. You need to combine your technical knowledge with your creative enthusiasm to produce the best results.

PHOTOGRAPHY AND PHOTOGRAPHS

If there is one element of scrapbooking that's universal, it's the photo, and, in turn, photography. I'll talk more in depth about photo-editing software and digital photography a little later in the book. For now, let's look at some ways you can get the most from your photos–from taking them to organizing your archives.

Take Your Best Shot

Great photos make great scrapbook pages. Whether you are taking photos the old-fashioned way with your handy point and shoot or your expensive 35mm with all its lenses, or the high-tech way with your digital camera, here are some basic tips to getting the best shot possible.

1. **Know your camera.** Read your camera manual and refer back to it if you have any problems. It is very important you know what all the buttons, selections, and features are and what you do to use them. Cameras have settings that help you take better up-close portraits or far-reaching landscapes. Cameras have buttons that adjust for available lighting, from a cloudy day to bright midday sun. By using the available technology, you will be rewarded with better photographs. Once you know how to use your camera, the best advice I can give is to practice as much as you can. This means keeping that camera handy for any and all photo opportunities.

2. **Create the scene.** Do more than aim and click your camera. Take charge and get the photo you want. As you look through the viewfinder, take time to really see what's going on. Ask people to move closer together for a better shot. Tell Grandpa Ralph to lean slightly to the left or right. Add a prop. Remove a hat. Do whatever it takes to make the photo better, tell a story, or, better yet, make you smile.

3. **Mighty light.** The most vital part of every photograph you take is the light. It affects the appearance of everything you photograph. Harsh light can make your human or animal subjects squint and grimace. Not enough light results in shadowy darkness in which details can be lost. If the lighting is not right, then move yourself or your subject. Check the settings on your camera and adjust for bright light, cloudiness, incandescent or florescent light, and moonlight.

If you are using a camera with film, film speed also affects the resulting exposure. Knowing you will have a day in bright sun photographing running children calls for a different film speed than a day of indoor flash photography capturing posed family groups.

Learn when to use your flash to fill in with light and when you should use your red-eye reducer. According to Kodak, the number one flash mistake is taking pictures beyond the flash's range. Photos taken beyond the maximum flash range will be too dark. As a general rule most cameras have a maximum flash range of less than 15 feet (xx m). You can find your flash range in your camera manual.

4. Eye to eye. One-on-one eye contact can bring a photograph to life. When taking someone's photo, remember to get to that person's eye level. This is especially important when photographing children. You may have to kneel, bend, or hunch, but the effort is worth it. Your subject doesn't always have to look directly at the camera, because by being at eye level you create a personal and warm feeling to the photo.

The background is beautiful, but the subject's smile becomes the focus of this shot by getting close to and level with the subject.

5. Get closer. When you look through your viewfinder it is natural for you to focus all of your attention on the subject. However, your camera isn't doing the same. Standing too far away can lead to your subject getting lost in the landscape or background. Move closer so you can see more detail. Or if your camera has a zoom lens, let the lens do the work. Next time you take a picture of your best friend, let her face fill the viewfinder, and you'll get some amazing results.

6. Keep steady. Nothing blurs a great photo faster than unsteady hands. Hold the camera with both hands and gently push the shutter button down. Taking a normal breath and holding it while you shoot a photograph can also help. You might also consider using a tripod.

7. Vertical vertigo. Most photos are taken with a horizontal frame. It's natural, and done without thinking. But why not shoot a photo vertically every now and then? Next time you get ready to shoot a photo, take a few extra seconds and turn your camera sideways. You might get a better shot. Many people or objects look better, like full-body shots or tall buildings, when you take a vertical picture. This also helps when you lay out your photos to create a scrapbook page-vertical photos add variety by giving you different lines, shapes, forms, and perspective.

8. Background matters. Keep your backgrounds free from clutter. A plain background brings focus to the subject you are photographing. When you look through the camera viewfinder, learn to pay attention to the area surrounding your subject. Make sure no trees grow from the head of your grandson and that no wires seem to stretch from Uncle Bill's shoulders.

9. Better off-center. It can become a habit to always put your subject in the center of your viewfinder and click, but centering is not always the best placement. Take time to play with shifting your subject to the left or right of center. Keeping the subject a bit off center adds to the variety of line, shape, form, balance, and harmony of your photograph, which in turn will lead to more exciting photos for your scrapbook pages.

10. Dramatic black and white. Since black-and-white photos are known to have a longer life than most color photographs and also produce a more dramatic effect, it's a good idea to include them in picturing taking. With standard cameras, this means purchasing black-and-white film. Some digital cameras have a grayscale mode that digitally reproduces the photos as black and white. Photo-editing software also has a grayscale feature that allows you to change a scanned color photo to black and white for printing.

The varying shades of gray in black-and-white photography create a drama of their own.

Organizing Your Photographs

A key to keeping the fun in scrapbooking is to always take the time to keep your photographs organized. Nothing is as overwhelming to a scrapbooker than seeing stacks of photos, which looks like a moun-

tain with a few foothills to most of us, or boxes of photos that have no rhyme or reason or organization in our work area. We tend to avoid the stacks in fear of being hit in the head by flying photos. Let's face it; you can't scrapbook with a concussion.

Schedule time to organize your photos. After a lifetime of organizing my own photos, I'm not going to promise that someday you are going to step back from your work area and realize that every single photo you have is not only organized, but safely at home in a finished scrapbook. But you can get control of the situation by spending time organizing your existing photos. Then you'll be prepared for all the new photos you'll be working with in the future.

Photos can be organized in two ways. The first way is to file by date or timeline. Start with your most current photos and work back in time. You can place the photos in envelopes, file folders, or other photo-oriented organizers and storage systems. Acid-free envelopes and file folders are available in most photo shops and craft stores. I prefer clear organizers because out-of-sight means I might not find what I'm looking for.

Why is organizing by date or timeline so important? Because that's the way we tend to look at things. We love to compare our fashion sense from our childhood or our teens to our more current savvy sense of style. We love to visually see how our children went from taking their

Photos can't be enjoyed when they're stored in a box. Getting them out and organized is the first step to creating great pages.

1985

first steps to how they looked while marching off to college or living on their own. It seemed to happen overnight, but our photos tell us it really did take 18 or 22 years.

A second way to organize is by event or subject. Place all your Christmas, family reunion, or vacation photos together in separate file folders. You can organize your photos by individual person-child, grandfather, or even family pet.

Or, you may come up with your own system to organize photos, one that works just for you. The key is to be able to find the photos you are looking for quickly so you can get on to scrapbooking. Whatever you choose to do, making the effort to organize your photos will save you time, and, most importantly, prevent you from losing or misplacing valuable photos.

Copying Photos and Copyright Awareness

At some point, you will need to copy some of your photographs for preservation purposes. These are usually older photos that no longer have a negative. Remember, you never want to crop or permanently adhere any photo that doesn't have a negative. You'll want to safely store the original in an acid-free environment and only use copies of the photo for your scrapbook pages. Later on, I'll tell you about scanning old photos (see page 18) so you can print them whenever you want from the convenience of your printer.

When you have copies of photos made at photo centers, the professional staff can make you aware that copyright laws protect certain photos, but when you are printing photos at home it may not cross your mind that you are violating these laws. With few exceptions, all professionally shot photographs may not be copied without permission from the professional photographer who took the photos. Some professional photographers do include a set of negatives with their paid service,

Preservation Copying

When scrapbooking, it's wise to never use an original photograph to create a scrapbook page unless you have the negative. Mistakes do happen, and the rule of archival preservation is never do anything to a photograph or vital family documents, such as birth certificates, marriage licenses, educational diplomas, or death certificates, that you can't undo. This includes cutting, manually cropping, writing on the front or back, laminating, folding, paper clipping, or stapling.

You can have photos and documents professionally copied, or you can use your home scanner or digital camera to make copies. Originals should be stored in an acid-free envelope, folder, or organizer and then kept in a safe place in a controlled environment. You want to avoid exposing the originals to direct sunlight, extremes in temperature, and high humidity. You should consider a fireproof safe or safety deposit box to hold original family documents and at least one photo of each family member.

but most do not. If you are given the negatives, you are given the right to make copies.

Some situations call for hiring a professional photographer—and a professional photographer is worth every penny. You don't have to worry if you'll get good pictures; whether the groom's head was out of the frame or that your finger blocked the flash. Take the time to ask up front the cost of reprints or additional prints you feel you might need for your scrapbooking. Make sure you set aside some of your budget for the photographs.

To avoid copyright problems altogether with professional photographers, take your own photos. Place disposable cameras on the table at a wedding, or ask several friends to take photos at the wedding for you. Learn to take casual headshots of your children for scrapbooking, saving the profes-

Using personal snapshots not only avoids copyright laws but also provides your scrapbook pages with precious everyday memories.

sional shots for framed presentations. While these types of photos may not be as perfect as those taken by a professional, you will own the copyright to your own work.

Some older photographs taken by professionals may no longer have copyright protection. If photos are over 75 years old, generally the copyright has expired. A professional photographer or photo printing shop will be able to help you determine if your photo falls into this category. Many times the photographer and/or his business are no longer available. Better safe than sorry. Try to locate the photographer and/or business. You can learn more about copyright protection and laws by contacting the Library of Congress:

Library of Congress
Copyright Office
101 Independence Avenue, S.E.
Washington, D.C. 20559-6000
(202) 707-3000
http://www.copyright.gov

DESIGN BASICS

Creating an attractive scrapbook page is like creating any other type of art. You need to use design elements and principles to help you create a page that is pleasing to your eye. You may be working on your 100th scrapbook page or your 10th without even knowing that you've included some of these important design elements and principles.

If you are not happy with some of your finished pages, you might want to review the following information to help you understand what you might be able to change to make the page more appealing. You'll also use these design elements and principles when creating digital elements for your scrapbooking pages.

Many scrapbookers feel the need to fill every inch of space of a scrapbook page with photos, journaling, and memorabilia. The page ends up being too busy to be pleasing to the eye. The photos get lost in the mess. Understanding the design elements of line, direction, size, shape, and texture can be of great use as you gather up your photos, decorative papers, and memorabilia. You should be aware of how using these elements properly can help coordinate all your scrapbook elements rather than making the mix clash.

One of the most common challenges for scrapbookers is color selection of papers. How do you figure out what other colors can be coordinated with a red background paper or the yellow selected for matting the photographs? Few of us are born with natural color sense. Understanding color and color theory can be helpful to overcoming this problem.

Elements of Design

Every element of design should play a role in the construction of your scrapbook page. Being aware of, and understanding each element, will help you create scrapbook pages with ease. They will help you pinpoint exactly what is wrong with a page that makes you unhappy and how to correct it.

- Color
- Intensity
- Value
- Line
- Direction
- Shape
- Form
- Texture
- Size
- Space

Warm colors   *Cool colors*

Color

Color is produced when light strikes an object and reflects that light into our eyes. Color is simply the name given to a specific hue such as peacock blue or goldenrod yellow. Colors are described as warm or cool. Warm colors are yellow, orange and red. The colors of blue, green and violet (purple) are considered cool. Warm or cool colors work well together, and combining a warm color with a cool color can help accent or highlight a photo or piece of journaling on a scrapbook page.

Color coordination is one of the most important elements of your overall scrapbook design. If you aren't happy with your color selections, you should invest in a color wheel. The color wheel is divided into three main categories: primary, secondary, and tertiary. The three primary colors are red, yellow and blue. These colors are used to create all other colors. By combining two of the primary colors, three secondary colors are formed, orange, green and violet. Combining a primary

and an adjacent secondary color on the color wheel makes the six tertiary colors. These colors are red-orange, red-violet, yellow-green, yellow-orange, blue-green and blue-violet.

Contrasting colors will draw your attention.

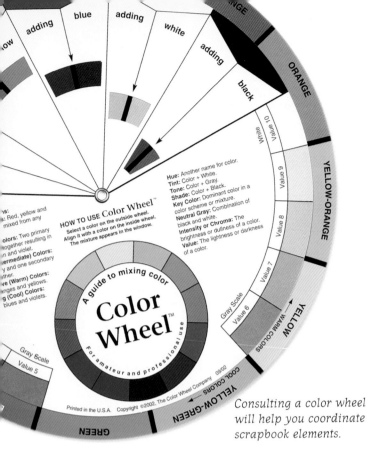

Consulting a color wheel will help you coordinate scrapbook elements.

What has been studied about color theory fills dozens of books. If you want to learn more about color theory you can find additional reading selections in the appendix.

Intensity and Value

Intensity describes the strength of a color. For example, the intensity of red can vary from the bright red of a clown's nose to the dull red of a maple leaf in fall. Value relates to how light or dark a color appears. The light blue of the sky on a sunny day has a different value than a deep-blue sea. You want to coordinate your color intensity and value. Most color wheels incorporate these two elements as well as color.

Line and Direction

A line is defined as a continuous mark made on a surface that can vary in appearance. A line can have length, width, texture, direction, and curve. The five directions of lines include vertical, horizontal, diagonal, curved, and zigzag. You will see lines and directions within your photographs, in borders and frames, within patterns of decorative papers, and within the overall finished page.

Figure 1. Using a zigzag as the guideline for your page layout provides direction and interest.

Shape and Form

A shape is two-dimensional and encloses space. Think of a circle, square, rectangle, or triangle. Shape is geometric, man-made, or free form. Keep in mind that shapes can have underlying meanings, such as the upside-down triangle that reminds us to yield or to take notice. You'll find shapes in your photographs, lettering, fonts, decorative paper patterns, die cuts, and other scrapbooking supplies. Forms are three-dimensional shapes, expressing length, width, and depth.

Figure 2. You can use different shapes and forms on a page.

Balls, cylinders, and boxes are forms. Make your shapes and forms work toward coordinating and accenting your scrapbooking page.

Textures add variety.

Texture

Texture is the surface characteristic or feel of an object. Adjectives like smooth, bumpy, shiny, glossy, rough, and soft describe textures we see around us. Textures may be actual if you include memorabilia on your scrapbook pages or implied through your photographs. Texture can add emotion, appeal to our five senses, and make scrapbook pages have a dimensional feel.

Size

As you gather all the different photos and create titles and captions for your scrapbook pages, you will discover that each may vary in size or all may be relatively the same size. It's important that you incorporate different sizes because photos, titles, memorabilia, and journaling that

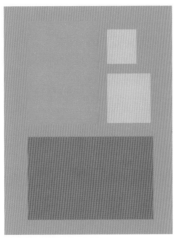
Figure 3. Varying the size of each element on a page helps lead the eye to the major focal point.

are the same size make a page look flat and boring. A pleasing blend will add interest and variety, making for a livelier page.

Space

Avoid overcrowding your page, or it will end up looking cluttered and busy. Although you may want to fill *every* space on a scrapbook page, you do need to leave some space open. This blank space, or white space as it is known, often helps feature or highlight a photo or journaling.

Principles of Design

Once you know the elements of design, you can apply them to your scrapbook page using the principles of design. Don't let the fancy wording intimidate you. As a child, you learned to tie your shoes by breaking the process down into steps and then using each step to form a finished bow that kept your shoes from falling off. Today, you just tie your shoes without much thought. The principles of design can become that easy too. Four principles that are useful to scrapbooking are:

- Contrast
- Proportion
- Balance
- Harmony

Contrast And Proportion

Using contrast in your scrapbook pages prevents all the components from blending into each other. Contrast can be achieved by combining different sizes, shapes, lines, or colors. Contrast isn't meant to distract the eye, but to guide it from one element to another on your scrapbook page. It's not about emphasizing one part over another, but rather helping to guide the eye through the page so nothing is missed. Often it's your photo

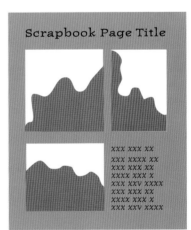
Figure 4. Look for the dominant lines in photos to give your page pleasing contrast and proportions.

that leads the eye. If you let it stand out from the title, captions, or journaling, the eye will first focus on the photo, then slide down to read the caption.

Proportion is the relationship between elements on your page in regard to size-how you place photos, memorabilia, and journaling on the background paper. Shapes can also play a role. Proportion can be balanced with contrast or unity.

Balance and Harmony

Balance means equalizing the weight of the elements of your design. A formal balance means that all the parts of your scrapbook page are of equal weight and are placed symmetrically. You achieve informal balance when you vary the value, shape, size, and location of your page's elements, which most often leads to an asymmetrical design.

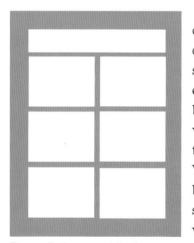

Figure 5. A symmetrical placement of elements creates a formal layout.

Harmony, or unity, gives the sense of all elements belonging or working together. Your scrapbook page should be viewed, or seen, as a whole, not just random parts thrown onto a page. You can do this by not overwhelming a page with too many shapes, lines, colors, or textures. If a page is too busy, it often means that there is no harmony between elements.

About Albums

Whether you create on 8½ x 11-inch (21.3 x 27.5 cm) or 12 x 12-inch (30 x 30 cm) pages, you have several styles of albums available to you. The album can be as simple as a three-ring binder or as elaborate as a leather-bound spiral.

Three-ring binders are versatile and easy to use. Choose a binder that is oversized to accommodate sheet or page protectors. Many scrapbookers recommend D-Ring style binders to keep pages flat, but the O-ring style will make page turning easier.

Advantages:
• Album can be expanded
• Pages lie flat when opened
• Pages can be removed and moved around very easily
• Available in different cover styles

Spiral binders are wonderful albums for single themes. Be aware that not all spirals are acid free, so choose carefully.

Advantages:
• You can often decorate the cover
• It includes both binder and pages
• Pages lie flat when opened
• Some page protectors slide onto page

Flex-hinge binders have a plastic strap binding that allows your albums to expand and your pages to lie flat and side by side. Look for pages that are heavyweight, acid free, and lignin free.

Advantages:
• Album can be expanded
• Pages lie flat when opened
• Page protectors are available
• Pages can be removed or moved

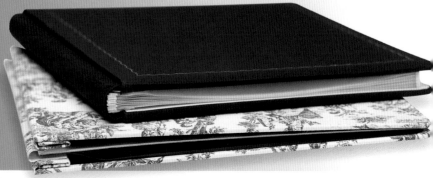

TOOLS OF THE TRADE

Don't throw out all those wonderful tools you've been using in traditional scrapbooking! You'll be using all of your favorites as you add digital elements. The only exception might be when you choose to create some totally digital scrapbooks or slide shows, but even then you might be surprised at how our traditional scrapbooking tools have a role to play in creating these projects.

You'll still need these basic supplies and tools:
- Plain and decorative acid-free papers
- Acid-free adhesives
- Photo albums, mini-scrapbooks, or journals
- Page protectors
- Paper punches
- Circle or shape cutters
- Decorative scissors
- Ruler
- Craft knife
- Scissors
- Rubber stamps
- Acid-free inks and inkpads
- Acid-free markers and pens
- Templates and stencils
- Coloring tools-pastels, chalks, watercolors, gel pens
- Embellishments

- Die cuts
- Stickers
- Eyelets
- Tags
- Brads
- Fibers, yarns, or floss
- Buttons
- Wood cutouts
- Wire or metal
- Memorabilia and ephemera

CHAPTER 2

Know Your Computer

What do hard drives, serial ports, USB, and RAM have to do with scrapbooking? If you've been afraid to introduce digital elements to your pages because all this sounds like a foreign language, don't despair. Taking a little time to get to know your computer's components and how each operates can open a new world of scrapbooking possibilities.

This book will describe all computer and digital components in generic terms; it will not matter which system you use. All projects can be adapted for use on a PC or a Mac.

HARDWARE

As well as coming in all shapes and sizes, a computer system can be one of two distinct types—a PC (personal computer) or Mac. Originally, PC was short for a personal computer manufactured by IBM Corporation, but now is a generic term for any computer other than a Mac, which is manufactured by the Apple Corporation. The main difference between PC and Mac is their operating systems that determine the format (platform) for their programs. Both types of computers can give you wonderful results for your pages.

What You'll Need

Whether you use a PC or Mac, both types of computers can be used to create scrapbook elements, pages, and even totally digital scrapbooks. To use this book effectively, or in other words to complete every project, you will need the following:

HARDWARE:
- Computer
- Flatbed scanner
- Color ink-jet printer

SOFTWARE:
- Word processing program
- Photo/image-editing program such as Microsoft PictureIt!, Adobe PhotoShop or PhotoShop Elements, or Paint Shop Pro.
- If you have a digital camera or want to use a digital camera, you will also need a spare USB or serial port to download the digital images into your computer.
- Some programs will come already loaded when you buy your computer, and most add-on devices like a scanner will come with software that must be loaded into your computer. If you are shopping for software, you may only need an abbreviated program such as PhotoShop Elements rather than the full-blown PhotoShop, which is more suitable for advanced or professional applications. Do a little research before shopping, then go with a list of questions to help you decide what is right for you.

Every computer has an operating system. It is the master program that runs automatically when you switch the computer on and continues running till you switch off. It is responsible for the many routine tasks required to keep a computer running, like moving the cursor when you move the mouse, providing icons and menus, running other programs such as a word processor or a game, controlling the various disk drives, the screen, and so on. The most widely used operating system for PCs is some form of Microsoft Windows including Windows 95, Windows 98, Windows 98SE, Windows ME, Windows XP, or Windows NT.

Since most of us have desktop computer systems, I will detail the components that make up a desktop system. However, there are other options available to scrapbookers. For practical purposes, those with limited space or those who travel may prefer using a portable laptop or notebook computer.

Even though it is more compact, a laptop still contains essentially all the components that will be described for the traditional desktop computer system. There are also smaller laptop computers called notebooks that are even more lightweight.

Because these smaller computers are portable, they are great for scrapbookers on the go. You can keep a travel journal, quickly view and store your digital images, or create and send pages to family and friends from any corner of the globe. Keep in mind that laptops and notebooks can be hooked up to other supporting devices like a scanner, printer, or even a digital camera. You can also hook up a full-size monitor and keyboard. But the result of adding all those to your portable computer makes it, in the end, look an awful lot like a desktop computer.

Laptops seem to get smaller and more powerful with every generation.

Considering Compatibility and Capability

Since there are many manufacturers of computer components and software, you want to make sure your system parts are compatible—some components are universally compatible, others are not. Software designed for a PC will only work on a PC, and software designed for a Mac can only be used for a Mac. Before you buy any computer system, printer, scanner, modem, digital camera, or software, know what you want to do with it and ask questions of the sales staff. Internet websites and computer magazines do a fine job of explaining how computer systems interact and work.

Though it sounds simple, you want to make sure the item you are buying is capable of doing what you want it to do. If you want to print off the page (or without borders), you need to know which printers offer this feature (there are only a handful that do). Or, you may only want to use a digital camera to send photos to your family and friends via e-mail or website. In this case, there is no need for you to buy the most expensive digital camera with a high-pixel capability—you can save money by finding out the pixel capacity you need before buying the camera.

Make Do or Upgrade?

Every time you turn around there seems to be another advertisement for an upgrade that promises to keep you current with new technology. However, you don't have to have the latest and greatest to get excellent results and create brilliant scrapbook pages. Many of the projects in this book are done with a basic computer system and common software.

Once you find that you enjoy using your computer for scrapbooking, you'll want to invest in expanding or upgrading your home computer system so you can stretch your skills. You'll find that

you will have fun investigating new ways to create effects and dynamic scrapbook pages.

COMPONENTS

In general terms, the main hardware component of a computer system is a computer chassis, usually a tall metal box, the tower case, or a small rectangular metal box, the desktop case. Inside this box is the guts of your computer, including the computer's motherboard with central processing unit, random access memory, hard disk, compact disk read only memory drive, compact disk re-writable drive, power supply, and internal modem.

The back of the box has all the sockets and connections to plug in external parts that complete your system, such as the monitor, keyboard, mouse, and printer. Last, but not least by any measure, are various memory units and acces-

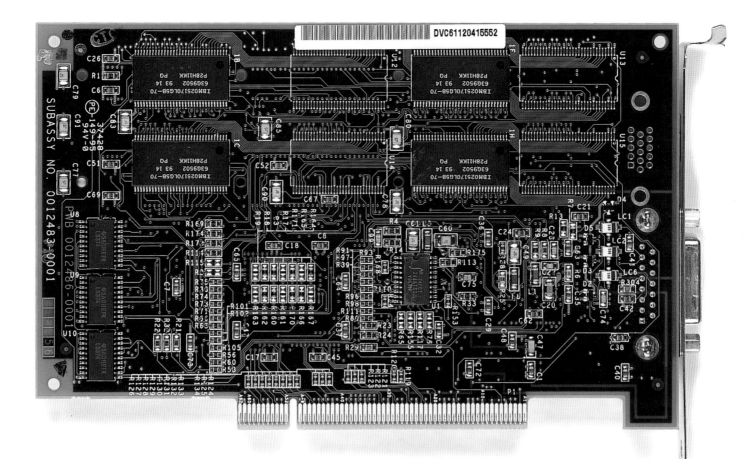

sories that can be used by the computer, such as a zip drive for storing large quantities of information on a zip disk, microphones for recording sound, and cameras for recording images.

A Peek Inside

Let's take a closer look at elements of this complex system called the computer. We'll start with the insides, those parts you can't see but are the workhorses of the system, and work our way out.

The motherboard is the main circuit board in the computer. All the pieces and parts of your system plug into the motherboard to make them work as a unit. The motherboard is partnered with a central processing unit (CPU), which is considered the nerve center of a computer.

The central processing unit (CPU) is also referred to as the processor. One of the most recognized CPUs is the Pentium.

Memory is a broadly used term for any device that holds information in your computer. This can be RAM, disk drives, CD drives, or DVD drives. (For more on memory, see page 27.)

Random access memory (RAM) holds the information you are currently working on. If you lose power, or if your computer crashes, you'll lose all information held in RAM—this is why you should get in the habit of periodically saving files as you work. With RAM, the more you have, the more you can do, such as open larger picture files or run programs simultaneously. Most computers have extra slots for adding more RAM.

Disk drives have heads that can write or read data on a disk or removable diskette. They are usually named or identified by the computer as C: for hard disks, and A: or B: for your main external memory choice which can be a diskette or CD. All you see on the hardware of your computer is the slot of the drive.

The floppy disk was the first type of removable storage that allowed scrapbookers and computer people to easily exchange data. This type of disk is now becoming obsolete and is being replaced with a Compact Disk (CD) drive that holds the amount of data equivalent to 500 floppy diskettes.

The hard disk, or drive, originally named to distinguish it from floppy disks, is your computer's main storage for programs and data. All computers are fitted with at least one hard drive.

The compact disk–read only memory (CD ROM) drive can only read preset data stored on a CD. Read only may seem restrictive, but it allows you to safetly install most programs onto your hard drive without altering data while doing so. It is usually named or identified as D: by the computer.

A Compact Disk–Recordable/ ReWritable drive (CD–R/RW) is essential if you want to share your scrapbooking via CD. It can read compact disks for data and can also create (burn) compact disks, including both audio and data. There are two types of media used by this drive. The CD-R disk can be written (burned) only once. You can't add or delete data once the compact disk is burned. A rewriteable compact disk format called CD-RW allows for adding or deleting information. They cost more than a CD-R disk but can be useful if you frequently modify and save pictures.

The digital versatile disk drive (DVD) is an advanced version of the standard CD drive, since DVDs are capable of holding far more information. Some new computers include this as standard equipment. DVD drives also read compact disks.

A digital versatile disk with a writable format (DVD RW) is a DVD drive that can create (write or burn) rewriteable DVDs in addition to being able to read DVDs and CDs. This is a still-emerging technology with the several formats— -R, +R, -RW, +RW, and RAM—that are not compatible with each other. Since there isn't a standard DVD writing format yet, you may want to wait to purchase this type of drive until a standard is reached on the media format. Just as CDs are replacing diskettes, and diskettes replaced floppies, in a few years the DVD will replace the CD, although some drives will support more than one format.

The power supply takes standard household power and converts it to the special lower power needed by computers.

An internal modem, the word taken from MOdulator DEModulator, allows computers to communicate over a phone line. It may be either an expansion card inside your computer or an external device plugged into one of the serial ports.

Making the Connections

When you find yourself needing inspiration for a scrapbook collage or some artistic craziness, all you have to do is take a look behind your computer chassis case.

However, there is a purpose to this seeming endless mass of snaking cords and wires. Connections are made by taking a connection cord from each component (like from your keyboard or printer) and plugging it into the right socket or port at the back of your computer chassis case.

A port is a socket on the back of your computer that allows you to plug in additional hardware such as a printer, microphone, mouse, or modem.

A serial port is a socket for plugging devices into the computer, such as an external modem or scanner. Most computers have two serial ports called COM1 and COM2.

A parallel port, usually called an LPT1, is the socket for plugging in your printer.

Universal serial bus (USB) allows you to attach extra devices to your computer. This port is much faster than a serial port and is used for high-speed scanners and printers. USB will eventually replace the serial port and parallel port on computers.

Completing The System

A computer without the output hardware to complete it is like having a brain without a body. A monitor, keyboard, mouse, printer, and scanner make all the internal processing come to life. There are also extra accessories to consider that add to the fun of working with your computer.

Monitors are needed so you can see all the great scrapbook elements and pages you are creating. Of all the things you buy for your computer, the monitor is one of the most important since it is what you look at the entire time you're using the computer.

Keyboards come in a variety of styles. It's a matter of personal preference whether to use a standard keyboard or an ergonomically split keyboard.

Printers allow scrapbookers to see the fruits of their effort. While there are printers that only use black ink, including laser printers and older ink-jet printers, most of us want to add color to our creativity. The color ink-jet and the photo ink-jet are the most economical color printers you can buy. For now, the color laser printer, most often found in commercial and business environments, is not affordable or really needed for home applications.

The mouse moves the cursor around on the computer screen. This little device is necessary for working in a windows environment.

The scanner is a computer version of a copier machine. This is the main device for getting our pictures, objects, and background material into the computer for digital scrapbooking. Instead of printing out a copy of an image or text, the scanner converts the image or text into a computer file. You can scan slides, transparencies, photographs, art work, and text documents. The scanner will record the various work in several formats like JPEGs, TIFFs, docs, which will all be explained as you continue to read.

Speakers can be built-in or external. While sound isn't really necessary for traditional scrapbooking, it's a wonderful feature for digital scrapbooks and slide shows. You can record your voice to play or enjoy music while electronically viewing your scrapbook pages.

A microphone allows you to record your voice, music, and other sound effects. It gives you one more dimension to explore and use to embellish your scrapbooking. You can create your own commentaries for scrapbooks, slide shows, or Web pages. If you enjoy adding the touch of sound, invest in a good microphone. Microphones are usually connected to your computer system at the front of the computer chassis.

MEMORY

Memory is one of the most essential factors in any computer system. Knowing how much memory your computer has lets you know which software programs you can install and run. And knowing about storage options lets you safely save or send those files containing your precious pages.

Different formats for saving photos/pictures, such as TIFF, JPEG, and BMP also affect the amount of memory you need. (See page 37.)

INTERNAL MEMORY STORAGE

A computer system has several key sources of internal memory. The most important is the hard drive, which stores information needed to run your computer and programs. This includes the software that enables you to create all the digital elements you will use in your scrapbooking. When you save anything, like a scanned photo or journaling page, by clicking the save button within the software, you are saving this information onto your hard drive.

For most, saving small bits and bytes of information isn't a problem. Today's computers have more than enough memory for average use. It's vital, however, to keep in mind that some software, such as photo-editing and graphics programs, need a lot of memory to operate.

EXTERNAL MEMORY STORAGE

When you've accumulated dozens or hundreds of files on your hard drive, what do you do with the ones you're no longer using but want to keep? And what about those times when you want to store your scrapbook pages or slide shows? At some point you will need to store information externally.

When this happens, you will need to use a diskette, compact disk (CD), and in some cases even a Zip disk. Since each digital element takes up memory, also referred to as space, on your hard drive, you will need to know how much memory you are using and how much you will need on the memory storage system when it's time to save your scrapbooking creations.

Memory by the Numbers

The quick review of memory that follows may come in handy when you're trying to figure out if you have enough memory left on your hard drive to load that photo-editing program, or if there's enough space on the CD to send your sister the digital scrapbook you've been promising.

Data is stored in bits and bytes

• Bit: The smallest unit of information in a computer and is either a 0 or 1.

• Byte: The most basic unit of measurement of information and is the space required to store one character. A byte is 8 bits.

• Kilobyte: 1024 bytes or characters.

• Megabyte: 1,000,000 (a million) bytes or characters

• Gigabyte: 1,000,000,000 (a billion) bytes or characters.

• Terabyte: 1,000,000,000,000 (a trillion) bytes or characters

Graphics include measurements of pixels and dots per inch.

• Pixels are, in most cases, small square dots. All computer screens or printed images are made up of pixels. The smaller the pixels, the higher the image quality.

• Dots Per Inch (dpi), a measure of picture quality, are often used to measure printer capabilities. The higher the dpi number, typically the better the quality.

Digital storage systems can hold different amounts of data.

• Diskettes hold up to 1.2 Mbytes. They are the most convenient and universal type of memory storage system for small amounts of information. A diskette can hold a few high-quality photos or several lower-resolution photos. It can hold numerous text documents like a travel journal or family tree. A diskette can be used over and over again. You can simply delete the information on a diskette and copy different information onto the disk. Diskette drives are no longer being installed in new computers.

• Compact disks (CDs) that allow you to store (burn) data are the recordable and rewritalbe disks (CD-R/RW), and will hold up to 800 Mbytes. A CD-R/RW will hold a digital scrapbook or slide show containing high-resolution photos, plus you will have enough memory to add sound to the scrapbook, including full-length songs.

• Zip disks hold up to 250 Mbytes. The amount of storage they offer makes them more suitable for business use rather than at home. You may use a zip disk to back up your computer systems information. Or, if you want to store several related all-digital scrapbooks together, you will need the storage capacity of a zip disk. Like the diskette, information can be added to or deleted from a zip disk.

• Digital camera memory cards can hold up to 5 Gbytes depending on the card. This is a type of disk that acts as the digital camera's film to capture images as data. To send the data to the computer, you remove the card from the camera and slide it into a card reader. You can transfer the photos into a folder on your hard drive for future use. A digital camera memory card is reusable. By deleting photos from the card, known as leaving it blank, you can use the card for taking more digital photos. Some newer printers have the capability to read the card and print photos without the computer. (See page 41 for more on digital cameras.)

• Digital versatile disks (DVDs) can hold either 2 Gbytes or 4.3 Gbytes of data depending on the format. Though it looks like a CD, a DVD uses newer technology to pack more bytes into the same space. The capacity of a DVD is enough to hold a two to three hour movie.

Back Up Everything!

It's a good idea to back up your system, especially your photos and journaling. To back up a system means that you copy files and folders from your computer's hard drive onto a diskette or CD. In the case of total system failure, or the corruption of a program, you'll be able to reload the information onto your computer.

SOFTWARE

Software helps make our computers powerful tools. By selecting, installing, and using the right software, we can do our taxes without using pencil and paper, we can send letters around the world electronically with a click of the mouse, draw simple illustrations without the need for 20 years of study and practice, print photos without a negative, hold libraries of our favorite music, or play a game of solitaire.

SOFTWARE FOR SCRAPBOOKING

Between the time I write this book and the time you read it, revolutionary software may come out that I can only dream about today. The software industry is aware of scrapbookers and their specific needs when it comes to using digital elements. Right now there is no one program that can do it all in one package. Using a combination of programs will give you the best results. For scrapbooking, you'll want to explore software in the following categories:

Word Processing and Journaling

Word processing programs come installed on most computer systems. Word processing was developed to help us communicate. In the good old days, word processing was done with a typewriter and the processing was done by the typist. Today, word processing programs help us edit, correct grammar, add graphics, turn black-and-white text into a rainbow of colors, and save all this work in a form that can be printed at a whim for years to come.

Journaling software focuses on creating titles, photo captions, and the stories we like to tell about the photographs on our pages. Instead of having to use complicated toolbars, journaling software does all the calculations for you. Page titles don't have to be a straight line of text. Journaling software lets you create titles that swirl

and curl and float. The only downside is that most journaling software doesn't include spell check, but the added creativity is worth double- checking for any typos. This type of software also includes the ability to shape your journaled words into recognizable silhouettes and outlines, such as a cupcake, stop sign, or leaf

Fonts

Your word processing software comes with a limited number of fonts. However, because fonts are some of the most fun you can have when it comes to scrapbooking, you can add more fonts by purchasing font program packages or downloading free fonts from the Web.

Photo Editing

There are several excellent photo-editing programs available. While each has its own unique way of operating, they share many of the same features, such as filters, red-eye removal, and resizing. Later, I will explain in detail some of the most important features you will use in photo editing for scrapboooking. Keep in mind that these programs tend to be complex. As you

progress, you'll need to plan time for reading your manual and experimenting with techniques. You can also find software for editing sound and video. This comes in handy when you are creating an all-digital scrapbook with voice and movie components.

Photo Printing

There are fairly simple programs that focus on how you will print your photos rather than photo editing them. Often this type of program is included with your printer for you to install on your computer, or is available through the printer's manufacturer. It can also be purchased from a software manufacturer. The best feature of this software is that it helps you lay out photos to print. You can select to print two 5 x 7-inch (12.5 x 17.5 cm) photos (either of one photo or of two different photos), three 4 x 6-inch (10 x 15 cm) photos (either all the same photo, two of one photo and one of another photo, or

three different photos), or a contact sheet of 25 images. Since you aren't just printing one photo at a time, you don't waste photocopy paper.

Templates, Clip Art, Borders, and Frames

Even though some word processing software comes with clip art, border art, and frames, the variety of graphics can be limited. You can purchase software programs that come with hundreds of graphics that give you an almost mind-numbing array of choices. In this category you will be

able to find software specifically designed for scrapbooking. Sometimes a manufacturer will package several types of elements, such as cut-outs, frames, decorative backgrounds, fonts, journaling, and titles. You can also find packages that revolve around a theme such as, weddings, baby, birthdays, and holidays. Many have pages that only need your photos to complete the page. All you have to do is print them out.

Scanning

This software comes with your scanner and is an interface that converts images to digital files, allowing you to bring the images into your computer. New technology is constantly improving scanner capabilities, such as the ability to fix minor flaws and color problems before importing the photos.

Music

To use music or sound in your digital scrapbooking, you have two options. The first is a WAV that converts a sound recording into a file that the computer can read and play. Since WAV files can be very large, sound recordings are often compressed into an MP3, which stands for a combination of MPEG 1 Audio Layer 3. An MP3 is the most popular standard for compressing audio and particularly music files down to a reasonable size with little or no loss of quality. You can download WAV and MP3 audio files from the web, purchase music already in the WAV or MP3 format, or use software to convert your own music from CDs into the WAV or MP3 format.

CD Burning

There are several add-on software programs you can purchase to help burn or record onto a compact disk that supports writeable CDs. The aftermarket software packages have simple menu selections that make burning CDs much easier than the software that may have come with your computer. Remember, you can't burn a CD using a CD ROM; this is a read-only drive.

Label Design

This software is often included in packages of labels you buy, or you can purchase software that helps you design labels-from address labels, to diskette labels, to CD labels. Label manufacturers often include a free software disk within the label package, but keep in mind that the software is usually designed specifically for that manufacturer's labels and will often not be compatible with all labels. You might also check the manufacturer's website, since most offer a free download.

Family History Software

If you've ever tried to trace your family tree, you know that the paperwork can be overwhelming with names, surnames, dates of birth, death, and weddings to record. Family history software can make this labor of love much easier.

Keep in mind the features that are important to you, and compare the software packages. The software shown below, Family Tree Maker, allows you to also incorporate photos and miscellaneous information.

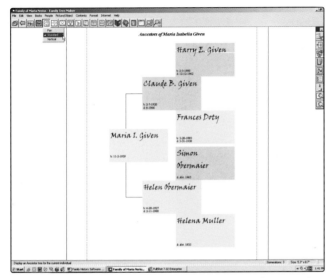

An ancestor's family tree is a very simple family tree of an individual, also referred to as a pedigree chart in genealogy. Using family history softwear makes organizing this information quick and easy.

INSTALLING SOFTWARE

Most software programs are stored entirely on your hard drive. You install the software using the manufacturer's instructions. But not all software needs a full installation. There are types of software that allow you to choose which portions of the program you wish to install.

As an example, if you are only going to use one or two pieces of clip art from a CD, there is no need to store the 300-plus pieces of clip art the program holds. All you have to do is access the program

from the CD, and install the sections you want. This allows you to save precious hard-drive memory.

As you gain more confidence in using your computer for scrapbooking, you'll want to add software to your system. Remember to check the system requirements of the software you are interested in and to make sure you have enough memory to support the program. The steps to install software are simple and most are formatted in the same way as explained here.

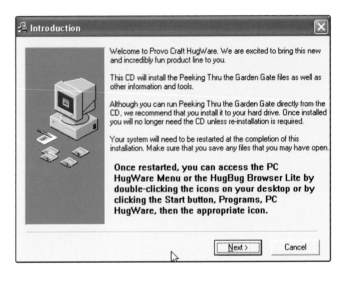

Insert the disk with your new software into the CD drive or diskette drive. In most cases the software installation program will open automatically. Click Next to start the installation. If it doesn't open automatically, find Open your CD or diskette drive (usually located within a folder called My Computer) to view the program, and double click on it to start the installation process.

All software will have some kind of user or license agreement. Read and accept the agreement. Next, you will see a screen that shows the computer automatically selected to install the program on the computer's C drive or hard drive. Note the Browse button. If you wish to place the program at a different location in your computer, you will click Browse to find the different location.

2 You can enter a different location and click OK. When you've decided where to place the program, click Next.

3 Some programs allow you to pick and choose how much you want to place on your hard drive. If you want to install all of the program, it is called a Full Install; if you want to select only parts of the program, it is called a Custom Install. After selecting Custom Install, the program asks you which part of the program you want to install.

4 The program will begin to install itself. Once installed, restart your computer to use the program.

Another option is to use software from a CD only. This means you do not install it onto your hard drive, but use it only from your CD drive. You should use this option with software you seldom use. You can also install software and use the program to create your elements, save the creations in a folder, and then remove or uninstall the program after you are done.

There may be times when you want to remove the software you are no longer using. Uninstalling software the right way is important—you can't just delete the icon on your desktop and have the software disappear. Make sure to use your control panel's Add or Remove option; you will delete the software from your computer, including icons and shortcuts, and free up the computer's memory.

Who Needs a Computer Anyway?

The development of new technologies will benefit scrapbookers who might want to bypass computers altogether. Newer printers include the hardware and software that allow you to simply slide your digital camera's memory card into the printer and print photos without the need for a complete computer system. Many digital cameras already include features that allow you to do simple photo edits of your images without the need for computer software. And who knows what the future may bring?

FILES, FOLDERS, AND ORGANIZATION

Software enables you to create information that needs to be stored on the hard drive or on an external memory storage system. A file in computer jargon is the raw data or information. Software programs are made up of dozens of files, and each photo or text document you store is a file.

With all those files floating around your system, you need a way to keep the files organized so you can quickly find that photo of Aunt Wanda or that cute border of ladybugs that is perfect for the page you are creating. Folders are used to organize the files. Windows, for example, predefines major folders for you: My Pictures, My Music, etc. This helps you and the programs you use place all your pictures in one place. You have the option to keep these folders or create your own.

This screen shows various folders organized in the My Documents folder. If I'm looking for photographs I click on the My Pictures folder.

Creating a Folder

An important step to installing and using software is to create folders to hold the items you want to store and save, such as downloaded fonts, enhanced photographs, or any journaling. The basic process to creating a folder is simple, but where you place the folder will be a personal preference. Often the computer will automatically locate a folder with a specific name in your C drive or hard drive, but you may want the folder located differently or name it differently.

For example, you may install a photo-editing program that you want located in your Scrapbooking folder rather than as a separate entry on your C drive. Or you may want to create a folder that can hold all your downloaded fonts.

Decide where you want to place the folder. This example used a location within the C drive or hard drive that is a location called My Documents.

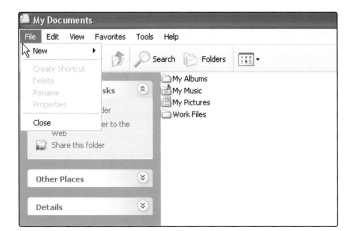

2 Click on File, and you will see in the list the word New. When you place your cursor on New, you'll see another list of functions. Find Folder and click on it.

3 A new folder will appear on your screen. Enter the name of your folder, and click. You've created a folder. Here I've created a folder for my digital scrapbooking.

4 You can continue to add new folders within the scrapbooking folder so you know where all your documents and photos are.

5 You can have more folders for organization within this folder. You must name each file with an original or unique name, and then do the same for each folder.

CHAPTER 3

Building Your Digital Scrapbooking Skills

Now that you have a basic understanding of your computer system and the digital tools available, it's time for the real fun! You can get started building your skills by working on creating digital elements in photo editing, word processing, and by using the printer, scanner, and internet.

WORKING WITH PHOTO-EDITING SOFTWARE AND DIGITAL IMAGES

Since photos are such a fundamental element of scrapbooking, photo-editing software is one of the most vital types of software scrapbookers can use. Most printers (and scanners) come with some basic photo-editing features, but to get the most features in one package you'll want a photo-editing program. You'll find numerous programs available that can make the photos you use in your scrapbook more exciting (see page 22).

Some programs are simple-helping you resize (make larger or smaller) your traditional film photos, or helping you arrange a better printing layout, such as two 5 x 7-inch (12.5 x 17.5 cm), four 3 x 5-inch (7.5 x 12.5 cm), or nine wallet-size of your digital photos so you don't waste photo-quality paper. Other programs are more complex-offering advanced cropping and photo-manipulation features.

These programs can include tools that allow you to adjust brightness and contrast, or remove color to create a black-and-white photograph. Some photo-editing software includes filter options that alter a photo in some amazingly creative ways, like turning the photo into a kaleidoscope or tile maze. Photo-editing programs can give you the ability to restore a damaged photo image or insert text directly onto a photo. The possibilities are inexhaustible.

BUT HOW DO I GET THOSE PHOTOS INTO MY COMPUTER?

Now that you're all excited about using photo-editing software, wouldn't it be nice to know how to get those photos into your computer? There are several ways to do this, but before we get into specifics, it's important to know that you will need to save or store most of your photos or graphics as JPEGs or TIFFs.

TIFF or Tat? Or Was It a JPEG?

The two most common types of formats for saving photos or graphics are TIFF and JPEG. You will find these options in your photo editing software, scanner, and digital camera. There are other storage options available, but for most of your scrapbooking needs, the TIFF (.tif/.tiff) or JPEG (.jpg/.jpeg) will be your best choice.

Remember how we talked about how important it is to know how much memory or space your information is taking or using? Here is one reason why: A TIFF (Tagged Image File Format) is a big file taking much more memory, usually up to 25 times more memory than a JPEG. JPEG stands for Joint Photographic Experts Group, the organization that standardized an image compression mechanism, meaning they figured out a way to make an image file smaller, allowing it to use less memory.

Keep in mind that:
• Saving a photo or graphic as a TIFF allows you the best resolution to print out that photo or graphic.
• Saving a photo or graphic as a JPEG allows you to store or send a compressed, thus smaller, file.

Smaller files, such as a JPEG, make it easier to e-mail them, upload them onto a website, post them on a mail list, or see them as a crisp electronic image on your computer screen without eating up precious memory space on your hard drive or a disk. The person on the other end of your e-mail will also appreciate your use of the JPEG format, since this type of file takes less time to download and open. If you've ever experienced a long delay while loading a web page because it contains heavy graphics, you know what I mean.

Photos or graphics displayed using a JPEG format usually pop up on your screen with little delay. Please note that some of that delay may also be caused by how you access the Internet. The rate-of-speed for dial-up access is slower than an DSL or cable modem. But we'll talk more about Internet access later in this section (see page 108).

How much memory you use will also play a role in determining which type of external storage system you'll need if you want to place your scrapbook page or entire scrapbook on an external disk like the diskette or CD. The more memory you use, the larger your external storage system needs to be. Only one or two TIFFs can be copied or saved onto a diskette, while you can save 50 or more TIFF photos on a CD.

Options for Converting Photos to Digital Images

Option 1:

Have your 35mm film developed, and ask your photo processor to place the photos onto a CD. Though you'll pay an additional fee above your standard photo processing charge for this service, it's worth it. Once you get your CD, insert it into your CD drive, then open the CD to see the photo files. This will give you access to the photos on the CD, but you will need to place the photos on your hard drive for photo editing. To do this, copy the photos to a folder. Once you've done this, remove the CD and store it as a backup or for future use. You can now access the photo files from the folder you've created.

Option 2:

Purchase a disposable digital camera. Just like disposable cameras loaded with standard film, you can now buy a digital version. After you take the disposable digital camera in for processing, you will get the photos back on a CD. Follow the steps in Option 1 for getting the images into your computer.

Option 3:

Take your 35mm processed prints to a printer who offers the service of scanning. The printer will scan your photos for you and place them on a CD.

Option 4:

Have someone send you a photo saved as a JPEG via e-mail. The JPEG is usually attached as a file to the e-mail. Download and save the photo. Notice that you should request a JPEG. You can ask that a TIFF be sent, but the download time can be measured in increments of hours rather than seconds like a JPEG. Also, keep in mind that some TIFF photo files are so large that most e-mail services can't handle the transfer and the e-mail cannot be sent.

Have someone send you a JPEG file (photo) as an attachment in an e-mail.

2 The JPEG will open in your default photo-editing software. At this time, you can photo edit the photo, such as removing red eye or correcting color balance. For this example, let's just save the photo as a JPEG in the computer.

3 Under File on your toolbar, you'll find the Save As button. Click on Save As.

4 This photo will be saved as Heather's Shower Viv and Marilyn in the My Pictures folder.

Option 5:

Use your own scanner to scan your 35mm photos. The scanner is one of the coolest tools used within a computer system. It is like a high-tech copier, but with more exacting definition and detail. Most scanners available are flatbeds, but be aware that sheet-fed scanners or all-in-one (scanner/copier/fax) machines can also be used for getting photos and images into the computer. We'll talk more about scanning later (see page 78). For now, let's focus on scanning your photos so you can work with them in your photo editing software.

When you lift the lid of a flatbed scanner you will see a large glass plate. Lay your photo on it and close the lid, then click for a pre-scan. You'll see the pre-scanned image on your computer screen. At this time, you'll select an area to scan. Selecting an area is much like cropping (see page 48). Your cursor becomes an adjustable box that allows you to define the lines within the larger scanner bed to only scan the selected area of your photo. Then click Scan. The finished scan can be saved as a JPEG or TIFF, which you can then print or send in e-mail. When using a sheet-fed or all-in-one printer/scanner copier, follow the manufacturer's instruction manual for handling the photo or image that my photo is not straight. I'll correct it, do another pre-scan before I actually scan the photo.

Open the scanner and place the photo on the scanning bed. Set your output resolution. For this example we'll use 200 dpi.

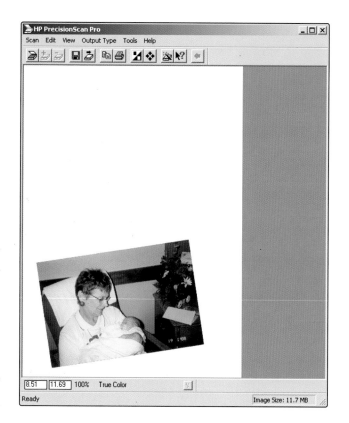

2 Pre-scan the photo. To allow you to make any adjustments before you actually scan an item, most scanners let you run a test (pre-scan). In this pre-scan, I see that my photo is not straight. I'll correct it, do another pre-scan before I actually scan the photo.

3 Once my photo is nice and straight, I'll highlight the selected area to be scanned and scan it. Then I'll save it in a folder by clicking under Scan and clicking Save As.

4 You can save the image in a TIFF or JPEG format. A screen box will appear when you click Save As that lets you place the photo in the folder of your choice, name the photo, and select the format. The example shows the photo going into My

Documents named, Ingrid And Nate, and saved as a JPEG. Now the photo is in your computer for future use.

Option 6:

If you have a web camera hooked up to your computer system, use it to take your photo. Note: This way is very limiting, since you can only take photos in front of the camera that is attached to your computer, and the resolution is not the best. This option served well before scanners and digital cameras became more commonplace. However, it is an option if you're on a small budget and mainly want to send electronic photos.

Option 7:

Take photos with a digital camera, and download the images into your computer using a card reader or direct connection to a digital camera. Since this is the best option if you are serious about using digital elements in your scrapbooking, it's time to discuss digital cameras.

SELECTING A DIGITAL CAMERA

A digital camera is a great investment if you love scrapbooking, but it is an investment nevertheless, so it's important that you get the right camera to match your needs. Digital cameras come in a vast variety of shapes, sizes, and features—you'll find low-end prices and some out of the world high-end prices. It's a good rule of thumb that the more pixels and more features a digital camera has, the higher the price will be.

You need to do some research and legwork before making your purchase. There are dozens of books, magazine articles, and websites that can give you basic information and comparisons, but the bottom line is how comfortable you are with the camera you decide to purchase.

You also need to be aware of how you plan to use your digital camera. You may only want to record and store the photos you take in electronic form for sending in e-mail, uploading to your family website or home page, or to be viewed from your computer. If you don't plan to use your digital camera to print photos, you don't need to worry about pixels. However, if you plan to print images, you'll want to have as many pixels as you can afford.

If there is one near you, locate a full-service photography store that sells digital cameras. You can find digital cameras for sale at most computer stores and some large discount stores, but I recommend the full-service store. Usually you'll find a sales clerk at this type of retailer who is also a well-versed photographer. Most importantly, ask questions! There are no stupid questions when it comes to purchasing a digital camera.

Questions to ask:

- How many pixels does the camera have?
- What are the best features of the camera?
- Does the camera come with any software?
- Can you add different lenses to the camera?
- What size memory card comes with the camera?
- Does the salesperson have a preference or use one of the models in the store?
- Does the camera come with accessories, and, if not, what accessories are available for the camera?
- Does the store offer a class for beginning and advanced digital photography?
- Does the camera come with a lens cover?
- Does the camera come with a basic case?
- What type of batteries does the camera use? Will you need to purchase specialty or manufacturer brand batteries?

It's important to hold the digital camera you're interested in. All cameras are shaped differently and have variable weights. Make sure you are comfortable gripping the camera. Can you easily find and press the buttons? Can you see the image in the monitor clearly?

Digital Camera Memory

Most digital cameras use a small digital memory card, but there are a few exceptions. The first exception is when the camera writes directly to a floppy disk or mini CD that is placed inside the camera. The floppy disk or CD system is used for simplicity. When you have taken your photos, you take the disk out of the camera and plug it into the appropriate slot in your PC tower. However, floppy disks can't hold many photos taken at high resolution. You either have to be near your computer so you can constantly download the photos before deleting them so you can reuse the disk, or you need to carry several floppy disks with you. CD-based cameras typically hold 50 times more data than a camera that uses floppy disks.

A camera with a digital memory card can come in all different formats, Compact Flash, PC Card, Secure Digital, and Memory Stick to name a few. Sizes range from 8 Mbytes up to a whopping 1 gigabyte (128 times bigger than the 8 Mbyte cards). The important thing to remember when selecting a digital memory card format is to use one that is widely available and compatible with your computer system.

Pixels

In traditional photography, the camera records images on film. In digital photography, the camera's computerized memory card records the images. In a photo taken with a 35mm camera, the picture is made up of thousands of dots. All these dots smash together to make up the image you see. In digital cameras, the tiny elements that make up a digital image are known as pixels.

Pixels can be all kinds of geometrical shapes, with each manufacturer tending to have a distinct shape for their pixels. Millions of pixels are needed to form or create the image. Because it takes so many, the term megapixels, meaning millions of pixels, is used. A digital camera is categorized in terms of its megapixel capacity. Although profes-sional photographers use digital cameras with 5+ MP (megapixels), most of us amateurs get great results with more affordable 1-2 MP cameras for electronic use, and 3-4 MP for printing images.

Resolution

Resolution is another important term to understand when it comes to digital photography. Image resolution refers to the intensity or concentration of detail an image will have based on the number of pixels used to create the image. The more pixels available and used, the higher the image resolution will be.

You can control the resolution of the photos you take by inputting your resolution needs into your digital camera. Resolution is often referred to as image quality, and can be found in one of the camera's menus. Most digital cameras offer three to four options for image quality:
• Basic to regular/normal resolution, which is sufficient for electronic photos (those used on web sites, e-mails, and digital scrapbooks/slideshows)
• Medium or fine resolution, which is fine for printing out photos
• High resolution, which is best for printed media (printing a photo or publishing in a magazine). Check out what resolutions are offered on your camera.

Select a lower resolution when the quality of your pictures is not critical—it will save memory space on your memory card and allow you to take more pictures. When image quality is critical, select a higher resolution, but be aware that you'll be able to take fewer pictures before your memory card is full. The difference in memory requirements can be quite dramatic.

Be aware that it's not possible to get a high resolution photo when a digital camera is set on Auto. This setting gives only a medium to low resolution depending on the camera. Even if you think you've set the camera for High/Fine resolution, the camera will reset when placed in Auto.

Using a Digital Memory Card

The digital memory card is the film of your digital camera. Just as traditional film comes in 12, 24, and 36 shots per roll, there is a similar comparison to the amount of shots when using a memory card. For example, a 3 MP camera with 40 MB memory card will hold 99 basic, 50 normal, 25 fine, and 4 high-resolution images. Or, when using a bigger memory card, like 128 MB, it will hold 318 basic, 162 normal, 81 fine and 13 high-resolution photos.

To copy digital images from a memory-card camera, you will need a card reader. This is a small device that you connect to one of your ports. You insert the card (with all your new photos) in the reader, which opens the card reader's program on your computer to give you access to your photographs. At this point, you are working directly with the memory card.

You can then copy or transfer the photos into a folder. Create a folder for the photos. Make sure the folder and card are both open and viewable on your computer screen. If you only want to keep one or two photos, highlight the photos you want to keep on the memory card and drag them to the folder. This process creates a copy of that photo in the folder. The original photo is still on the memory card. If you want all the photos—you'll edit and delete later—just highlight all the photos and drag to your folder.

Many photo-quality printers have built-in card readers, where you plug the memory card into the slot on the printer and access your photos in the same manner as you would with a self-contained card reader. The benefit of having a card reader within the printer is that you can print photos without even needing a computer system. Just remember that you will not have many, if any, options to edit the photo before printing.

Copying Photos Into Your Computer from a Memory Card

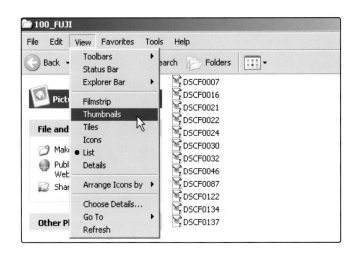

You'll find your photos labeled with sequential numbers. You can copy these numbered photos into a folder, then edit and rename. Or you can do this from the reader card, then copy into a folder.

An easier way to view a photo file is to use theThumbnail view. This sample shows the photo files as a List. Let's change it to Thumbnail.

locate the photo you wish to edit. In this example I'm looking in my holiday folder for a Christmas photo from 1998. I'll open the Christmas 1998 folder by clicking on it.

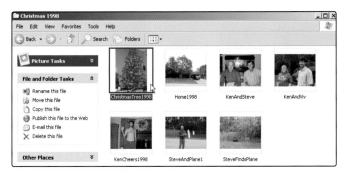

3 Here's the same photos viewed as Thumbnails. It's much easier to rename the numbered photos when you can actually see the photo

2 I found the photo I was looking for which was a shot of our Christmas tree. Click on the photo and the photo will be opened in your photo-editing program.

OPENING A PHOTO TO EDIT

Now that you have your photos in your computer, you are ready to begin working with them. Using photo-editing software is relatively easy, and the more you use the software the more options you'll discover. To do the most basic enhancement to a photo, open the software program, then open the photo file you've selected.

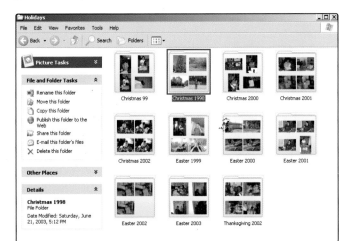

1 Open your photo-editing software. Click the File button to see a pull down menu. Click the Open button. This will open a new screen box that allows you to browse all your files and folders to

3 Once opened in the photo-editing program, you can edit the photo as you wish.

BASIC PHOTO ENHANCEMENT

You can experiment with the enhancing tools within the program to alter your original image to your liking. Once done, just save it, and your new enhanced photo is ready for use. Most photo-editing software packages include a shortcut or automatic enhancing that includes color balance, contrast, and saturation. All you have to do is click the auto enhance feature, and the software does the calculations and corrections.

As you get more comfortable with the software, you may want to manually adjust color, contrast, and saturation. What's the difference? When you manually control the adjustments by using the different enhancement dialog boxes, you use your own eye to decide when you think the photo is perfect. Auto enhancing takes seconds to perform, while manual adjustments can take several minutes to make.

A good way to think about the difference is to compare it to having film developed and prints made from 35mm. In most cases, your photos turn out okay, but in some cases you need to go back to the photo processor and ask that a photo be redone by either adjusting the color or contrast. In nine out of 10 photos, auto enhancing will do the trick; however, be aware that auto enhancing, and even manual enhancing, are no guarantee that a too-dark photo will become better visually—but in most cases you'll end up with a crisper image.

Different types of lighting, photographic equipment, and photo processing can cause incorrect coloring in images. Apply the automatic color balance feature to correct the coloring, remove any color cast (bias), and create natural-looking colors in your image. Use it for correcting images with several colors rather than for images with variations of one color. After you have corrected the color balance, correct the contrast and then the saturation of your image, if necessary.

The automatic contrast effect maximizes the visible information in an image to reveal all the detail and use all available colors. It adjusts the balance of the highlights, shadows, and the overall light and intensity of the image. Use the automatic saturation feature to adjust the saturation or intensity of colors in a photograph. The saturation of a color determines its vividness. Saturated colors appear bright and brilliant. As the saturation decreases, the colors appear subdued or washed-out. This feature has no effect on grayscale or black-and-white images because they have no color, but it can be used with sepia.

Beware Permanent Changes

Please note that no matter what photo editing you do, you need to keep the original photo file unaltered. This is important if you want to make other changes to the photo at some future date. Keep in mind that each time you edit or alter a photo, it creates some distortion, sometimes referred to as "noise". You can only edit or alter a photo to a certain degree before you begin to lose quality and resolution. If you keep altering a photo, you will reach a point where you will lose crisp printing quality and you can end up with a digital blob instead of an image. Always keep the original digital photo as a saved backup, and save the enhanced photo with some kind of new name or wording that lets you know the photo has been enhanced or altered.

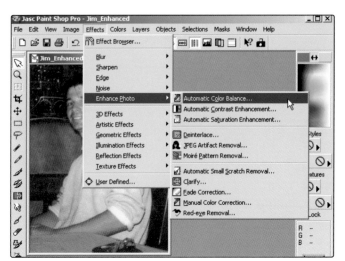

2
Auto color balance is the first enhancement you will do to a photo. All photo enhancements (auto and manual) are found under Effects.

3
Click for Auto Color Balance. A new screen box will give you some options about color balance. You can manually adjust or just click OK and the

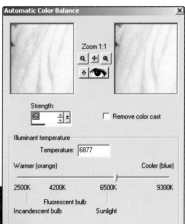

1
Open the photo in photo editing. The photo shown here was taken with instant film over 20 years ago—instant film was never as crisp or clean as 35mm. The photo has darkened over the years, altering the skin tone and creating a dark and unfocused background. I cropped the original (see page 48) to cut out as much of the dark background as possible. Let's see what photo editing can do to make this photo better. Note: This photo was scanned at a resolution of 300 dpi. Two hundred dpi was not good enough to photo edit, and the higher resolutions (600 or 1200 dpi) may show too many scratches on original older photos.

color balance will automatically adjust. Note the auto adjust wants to make the photo cooler (blue tones to take away the harsh red and ruddy tones). Auto color balance gives the photo more realistic color especially to the skin.

4 The next step would be to adjust the contrast. The photo shows an auto contrast. The auto contrast made the background even darker. Using this feature did not enhance my photo, so I opted not to adjust the contrast.

5 The final step in photo enhancement is auto saturation. This helps colors stand out. However, for my photo, I felt it made everything too red—although the auto saturation was excellent for the red velvet chair in the background. I chose to manually adjust the saturation.

6 This is the auto saturation dialog box. The photo editing program automatically selected Normal Bias, Normal Strength and did not pick up that Skintones were present.

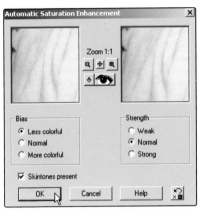

7 Manually, I changed to a Less Colorful bias (the whole photo had a muddy cast to it) and checked that skin tones were present in the photo.

8 I'm happy with the auto color balance and manual saturation. I didn't have a great photo to begin with, but the final result of photo enhancement gives a clear, clean realistic photo. You can still see some white flecks to the right side of the photo. Those are scratches that you can remove or fix-you'll find out how on page 60.

CROPPING

Traditional scrapbook cropping is done with a pair of scissors or craft knife and ruler. The cropping is permanent unless you like the look of a taped-back-together photo. Photo-editing software allows you to crop more effectively and with a less permanent result.

Open the photo in your photo-editing program. You'll need to find and select the cropping tool (in this case the cropping tool is located on a side toolbar). If you can't find the cropping tool, use your program's Help section.

2 Click on the cropping tool, and move the box until you are happy with the placement-the area inside the box will become the photo. Double click or select the Cut button. Anything outside the cropping box will be removed. In this photo I just wanted to crop away a little all around the edges to have the photo really focus on the faces.

3 Under Image you will find a Crop button. Click on it.

4 Here is the cropped photo. I'm not happy with it because I want the edges tighter around the subjects, and I cropped too much off the top.

6 Here is a tighter crop. I like it better for my scrapbook page.

5 Under Edit you will find the Undo Perform Crop. Click it, and you will go back to the original photo.

7 There are other ways to use your cropping tool. If you want a photo that just shows one family member or friend, you can take a group shot and crop down to one person. Using the same photo as above, I cropped each person individually starting with Cousin Berta on the left.

Cousin Berta

8 You can use a freehand cropping tool to literally cut out a person or thing within a photo. I zoomed in to get a better angle to make a freehand crop of Cousin Zenta.

9 Using the freehand cropping tool, I carefully drew a line around her head and shoulders. When finished, I was able to move the cropped image around the screen. This feature helps you see if you have the correct cropping line.

RESIZING AN IMAGE

You can make any photo larger or smaller than the original by using photo-editing software. The following example shows how to enlarge a small photo-you use the same steps to make a photo smaller, except you'll use decreasing numbers in inches or centimeters on the resizing screen.

I Open the photo you want to resize in your photo-editing software. You'll find that many older photographs are smaller than our standard 3 x 5-inch (7.5 x 12.5 cm) photos. Even though it looks large, the actual size of this photo is $1\frac{1}{2}$ x 2 inches (3.8 x 5 cm).

2 Under Image you'll find a pull down menu that has an option to Resize. Click on it.

3 The resize dialog box will let you choose to resize in pixels or actual print size (in inches). In this box you will always see the original size of the photo first.

4 Enter the new size for the photo. The program only allows you to enter width or height, not both-once you enter one measurement, the program will calculate the other. Click Ok and the program does the resizing.

5 Save the photo under a different name than the original. Remember to always keep a copy of the original photo without any digital enhancements.

A finished page using the resized photo

RED-EYE REMOVAL

Nothing can spoil a photograph more than red eye. Most cameras have red-eye reduction option, but just in case that fails, you can remove red eye in photo-editing software.

Open your photo-editing software. If you don't know where the red-eye removal icon/button is, you can find it using the software's help feature.

Open the photo needing the red-eye repair, then open the red-eye removal option. In this program I went to Effects, then Enhance, then clicked on Red Eye. Both individuals in this photo have noticeable red eye, one with brown eyes (left) and the other with blue eyes (right).

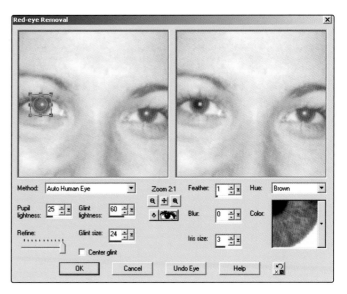

Zoom in on the face so you see eyes clearly. The image on the left is the one you work on; the image on the right shows you what the eye will look like after the red eye has been removed. You can enlarge or reduce the correction box by dragging its outer lines to better line up with the eye in the image. You need to select the eye color in the Hue box.

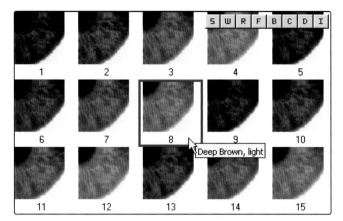

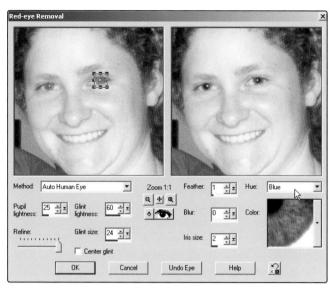

4 You can select from various shades of color for the iris. Within the hue you can select the intensity of brown you need. Working one eye at a time, use the red-eye removal box for lining up the pupil.

6 For these eyes, select blue as the hue, then select the blue that closely matches the girl's eyes. Correct the red eye just as we did for the brown eyes.

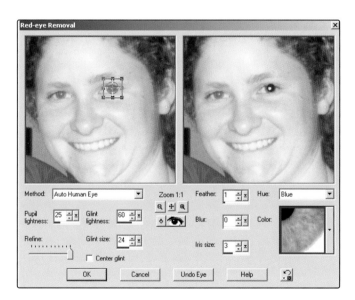

5 Before saving the altered image, let's correct the second set of eyes on the girl to the right who has blue eyes. Note that since this set of eyes is smaller, I will need to reduce the size of the correction box for a better fit.

7 This is the final result. Now our attention is drawn to their smiling faces rather than the glare of red eye.

Pet Eye

There is a difference between red-eye removal for people and for animals, which is known as pet eye. For animals, not only can you match the hue, you can select from different eye shapes.

I Open the photo needing repair in your photo-editing program. Select the red-eye removal feature. Click on Method, and you'll see a feature for pet eye. Select this feature.

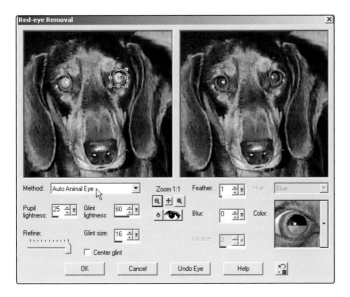

2 Zoom in on the eyes, position your correction box, and select the hue you need.

3 The finished photo is more appealing without the white-green glow of pet eye.

EFFECTS FILTERS

Using filters is a creative way to make unique background or decorative papers for your pages. A filter is an effect that, when applied to an image or part of an image, changes the appearance of the image. Filters can create fairly simple effects that mimic traditional photographic filters, which are pieces of colored glass or gelatin placed over the lens to absorb specific wavelengths of light, or they can be more complex to create artistic effects. You'll find filters in Paint Shop Pro, Picture It!, Photo-Shop, and PhotoShop Elements, as well as other photo-editing and graphic applications.

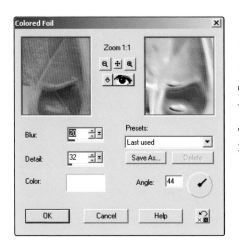

3 Most software will give you a preview before actually altering the image.

1 Open your photo-editing software. Open the photo you want to work on. The file/photo opened in this example is of a Chinese Elm branch from my backyard. (If you want to have fun using your own backyard or garden photos, see the project on page 84.)

2 Now you can apply a filter to the image. This photo-editing software refers to filters as

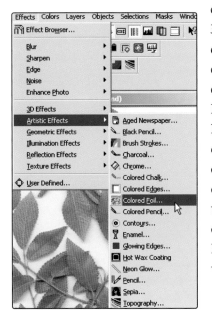

effects including 3-D effects, artistic effects, geometrical effects, reflective effects, and so on. Each category may have up to a dozen different kinds of effects. The first example was found under artistic effects. The Colored Foil filter or effect was selected.

4 If you like the preview, just click OK and the program will alter the image. This process may take a little time, but not more than 15 to 25 seconds. When done, you can see your image as Colored Foil.

5 Another example of a filter can be found under geometric effects. Curly Qs was selected.

7 And under texture effects we can select the Weave filter.

6 Under reflective effects, we can select the Kaleidoscope filter.

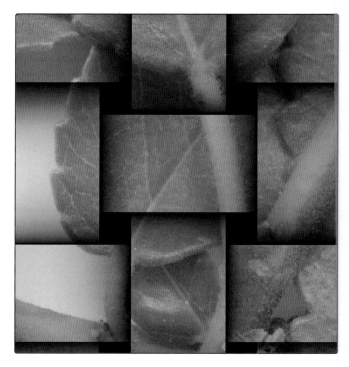

8 If you zoom in, you can see the image now looks like it is woven.

Once you find an effect that coordinates with your scrapbooking project, all you need to do is save the effect as a file, and print. I selected an elm branch because one of my favorite photo subjects is my garden or nature. You may have your own very different passions. So include what you love as a subject of a scan, and personalize your own background and accent papers that reflect how unique you are.

THE GREYSCALE EFFECT

Since black-and-white photos are said to have a longer life than color photos, you should always include a roll of black-and-white film in addition to your color rolls for all major events. If you just want the look of black and white, most printers have a feature that allows you to print a color photo in grey scale or black and white, which is preferable to just printing a color photo using black ink. The best option for turning a color photo into a black and white is to use your photo-editing software. Begin by selecting the tool option under Color.

2 Select greyscale. Hit the enter key.

3 The color photo becomes black and white (greyscale).

Open the photo-editing software. Open the photo file.

Greyscale Shortcuts

You can greyscale, which means turning a color photo into a black-and-white image, in several ways:

- Select the greyscale or black-and-white feature on your digital camera
- Scan a color photo in greyscale
- Photo edit a color photo with a greyscale filter or effect
- Print a color photo in greyscale mode

Sepia–Another Aging Option

You can age a photo using a sepia effect, which gives it the brown tone of an old-fashioned photograph. Most sepia filters or effects will have a hint of color to recreate the hand tinting that was done to older black-and-white photographs. Some photo-editing software will keep this slight coloring, while others will give you only the brown tones.

Aged 10 years

1   Open your photo-editing software. Open the photo file. Under effects you'll find a sepia option.

Aged 100 years

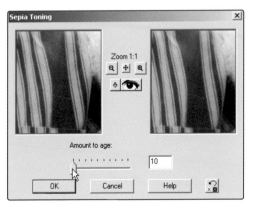

2   Sepia toning allows you to select how much you want the photo aged. Select the number of years to age, then click OK.

Aging a photo 100 years plus 10 gives you almost total greyscale or black-and-white results.

You can get interesting results adding sepia tones to an older photo. The colors in this photo faded unevenly leaving the red as the dominant color. I selected sepia, and first aged it 10 years. I finally settled on aging it 100 years to get the look I wanted for making my page below.

EFFECTS BROWSER

You may have an Effects Browser in your photo-editing software that enables you to scroll down a list of available effects/filters. This is like a mini toolbar that includes only effects options. Using the browser is a great way to quickly see what the effects and filters will do to your photo and provides a handy tool for experimenting—it's a fun way to see a lot of effects at a glance. Let's take a quick look at how to use the effects browser.

The original photo before any effects or filters.

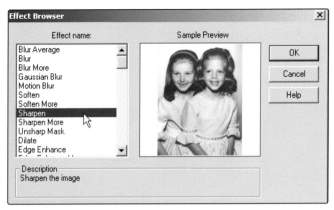

You can Sharpen the photo, giving you better detail and contrast.

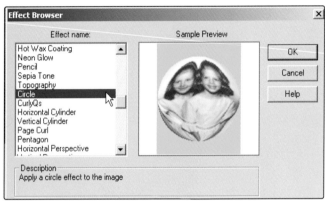

There are some silly effects like this Circle filter. Not a filter you'd use for most of your scrapbooking, but a fun way to express your creativity.

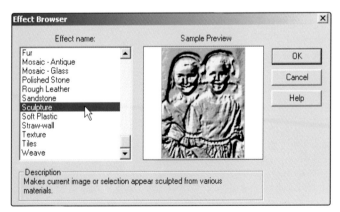

The Sculpture filter converts this photo into an artistic engraved reflection that would be great for the cover of a scrapbook or to use on a CD label.

RE-TOUCHING AND REPAIR

It is possible to retouch any photo and even repair older photos by using photo-editing software. The easiest way to make corrections is to use the scratch remover feature. Unlike the advanced correction tools, such as the ink dropper or airbrush feature where you have to perfectly match up the photo colors using the program's limited color palette, the scratch remover matches the colors for you automatically.

You work a very small area at a time, and the changes are very subtle. You can repeat the scratch remover process until you are happy with the results, which is unlike the very dramatic color changes that happen with the advanced retouching options.

Retouching

This photo shows a small but pesky piece of dead grass in the middle of my dog's face. On the otherwise perfect photo (no pet eye!), the spot of white is distracting on the dog's black coat and will be even more noticeable if I decide to enlarge the photo.

Open the photo-editing software, and open the photo to retouch. Select the scratch remover option on the toolbar. A small square will open when you place the scratch remover icon over the area you want to retouch. Keep repeating this process until the area is entirely removed.

2 The dead grass has vanished! Save the edited photo.

Repairing a Photo

In this example photo, which amazingly is a copy of a copy, there is a water spot beside my grandmother's head, a stain caused by oil from my fingertips on her blouse, and a true scratch on top of the water spot. Using the scratch remover feature we can remove these imperfections with little effort.

Select the scratch remover tool. Move the small screen box that appears over the areas that need correction. You are working only a small area at a time, so continue until happy with the finished results.

2 With the water spot, stain, and scratch removed, this is a much better photo. Remember to save the edited file before closing the program.

Key To My Heart

You don't need black-and-white film to get black-and-white photos. Use your scanner to magically turn color photos into dramatic black and white images. Making the images look older added to the overall appearance of this antiqued memory box.

MATERIALS

Photos
Old or faux postage stamps
Postage stamp envelopes
4 pieces of cardstock in a solid color
Large brass heart charm
Ribbon or floss, 10 inches (25 cm) long
Skeleton key
Cigar box
Brass word plate
Chalk inks in inkpads in goldenrod, brown, and dark green

SOFTWARE & TOOLS

Scanner
Photo-editing software
Printer
Scissors or personal trimmer
Acid-free adhesive
Ruler or measuring tape
Bone folder or scoring blade
Artist's sponge

INSTRUCTIONS

1. Lay your photo on the scanner bed. Select Output Type, then Grey Scale. The preview scan should now show the color photo in black and white. Save the image as a TIFF. Repeat this step until you've scanned all your color photos.

2. Depending on your photo-editing or printer software, print the altered photos one at a time or group several photos together, then print. Crop photos as needed.

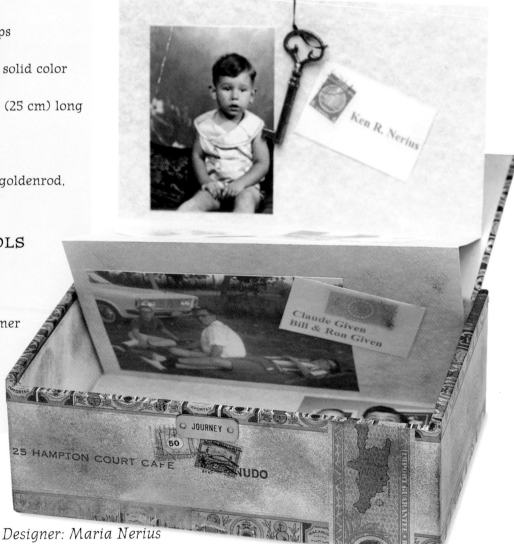

Designer: Maria Nerius

3. Hand print or computer generate the names of the people in photos. Trim so the names will easily slide into the postage stamp envelopes.

4. Note that on the project shown, the placement of the names vary, allowing you to place old or faux postage stamps in different places. Adhere the stamps to the name titles. Slip the name titles into postage stamp envelopes. Using a tiny dot of glue or tape, seal the envelope.

5. Place a sheet of solid-color cardstock in front of you. Measure 5 inches (12.5 cm) down from the top of the sheet, and score the paper using a bone folder or scoring blade. Measure another 5 inches (12.5 cm) down and score. This will give your two panels that are 8½ x 5 inches (21.3 x 12.5cm), plus a small flap that's 8½ x 1 inch (21.3 x 2.5 cm). Repeat this step for the remaining three sheets of cardstock. Crease the folds firmly.

6. Make a continuous cardstock sheet. Adhere one of the small flaps to the back of the next sheet's top. Repeat this step until you have one long sheet of paper with accordion folds that end with a small flap. Allow to dry completely.

7. Decorate the top panel of the cardstock sheet with old or faux postage stamps. Tie a small length of ribbon or floss to the brass heart charm, and adhere the charm to the center of the panel. Tie the loose end of the ribbon to the skeleton key, trimming the ribbon if needed.

8. Begin adhering the photos and the name envelopes to the panels of the continuous cardstock sheet. Adhere a few stamps to the inside and outside of the cigar box. Adhere the brass word plate to the front of the cigar box.

9. Antique or age the design. Using the artist's sponge and one of the chalk inkpads, tap the sponge on the pad. Tap the sponge on a piece of scrap paper to remove most of the ink, then begin tapping the ink onto the cigar box inside and out. You want to just lightly bounce the sponge over the surface.

10. As in step 9, sponge your embellished panels. Since the ink will not hurt your photos, you can sponge over the photos if desired. Repeat steps 9 and 10 with the remaining two colors of ink to create a layered effect. Allow the ink to dry completely.

11. Adhere the embellished cardstock sheet to the cigar box by gluing the last small flap to the bottom of the cigar box. Allow to dry. To see all the photos, just lift the key and watch the panels unfold.

WORD PROCESSING AND JOURNALING

Word processing software has a variety of options to use in your scrapbooking. With it you can...

- Create page titles or toppers
- Make an opening page for an album
- Create the look of hand lettering
- Caption photos
- Journal with *ease*
- Make a scrapbook index
- Create signature labels for your pages
- Keep a running record of pages created
- Store an inventory list of your photos
- Have the choice of a font size and color
- Boldface, italicize, and underline text
- Insert photos, graphics, borders, and clip art

The best part of using a word processing program is that you'll never need to use correction fluid to cover a mistake, worry that your caption lines are marching downhill, or figure out how to center a title onto a page-the software does it all for you.

Processing Words?

Word processing is an old term created before typewriters became obsolete and before computers became a household item. At one time you could buy a word processing system. It was a typewriter-like machine that had some memory capability and actually looked like a clumsy cross between a typewriter and computer.

USING TOOLBARS

A toolbar is a horizontal row or vertical column of buttons that gives you an easy and visual way to select certain functions available in a software program, such as printing a document, saving or cropping a photo, or getting the help menu for the software.

You will see a basic toolbar when you open your word processing program. As an example, clicking on the View button on this basic toolbar opens a pull-down menu that gives you even more options for toolbars that you can open and make visible on the screen. This word processing program has a total of 16 different toolbars that can be viewed as you use the software.

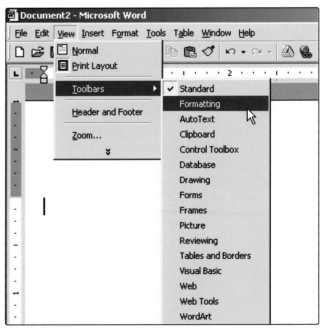

After Clicking on the View button, then again on Toolbars, this menu shows the toolbars you can view to help you in creating your pages.

Specialized Toolbars

The number of toolbars you have open is really your choice. When just typing in a title or simple caption, there is no need to have more open than your basic toolbar. If you want to create totally digital pages or create a web homepage, you might prefer to keep those toolbars open so the features you wish to use are visible while you work.

The Picture toolbar is a floating bar—you can move it anywhere around the screen—and lets you quickly insert a photo or graphic.

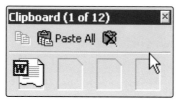

The Web Tools toolbar is also a floating one that lets you click on Web options (as in building, uploading, and editing Web pages.

Clipboard lets you cut and paste several different pieces of text or graphics. The clipboard holds the data until you clip on it and paste it.

The Control toolbar is a more advanced feature that gives you more control and options for word processing documents and presentations.

WordArt toolbar lets you use the WordArt feature (specialized Text graphics formats) with all the options clearly visible at one glance.

The Draw toolbar lets you draw arrows, lines, boxes, text boxes, and add color.

ASSEMBLING A TITLE

A fundamental element to a scrapbook page is the title, topper, or header. Word processing software makes creating a title quick, easy, and fun. I write like I should have been a doctor rather than a writer, so I find word processing gives me the added bonus of readable in my titles, captions, and journaling. You can experiment with font and size before you save and print.

Changing a Font

To begin, just type in the title. The font you see first is usually the default font. In this program it's Times New Roman in 12 point. To change from one font to another, you simply highlight your text, click the arrow to see the pull-down menu of fonts, and select a new font—you'll see the new font's name displayed in the font box, and next to it you will see the font's size.

Have some fun by typing out a line of text and changing the font until you find one you like or fits the mood of your page—this is a great way to get to know the fonts in your computer.

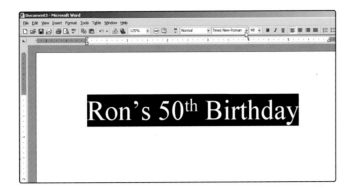

You can keep your word processed titles straight as an arrow or use features to give them dynamic shapes and effects. On the following screen I combined the steps for developing a title for a scrapbook page.

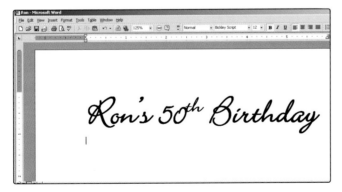

1. Type in the title. 2. Select a font and size—Pepeta MT in 36 point is shown above. 3. You can choose to boldface the type. 4. You can center the title on the page if you are creating an entire scrapbook page on the computer. 5. You might also want to add color to the title.

1 | Highlight the text you wish to change to a different font. If you don't change the font before you type in the text, the computer will use its default font, which is Times New Roman in this program.

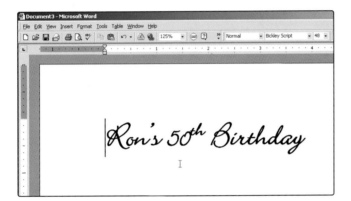

2 | After selecting Bickley Script, the font changes with the click of the mouse.

Once you're satisfied with the results, you're ready to print the title. From here, you can use traditional scrapbooking skills to trim, mat, and adhere the title to your scrapbook page. It's a good idea to save your work. Sometimes at your computer a title looks the right size, but when you trim and mat it, the title ends up too small or too big or not the right color or font. Save yourself some time and just save your work as a file. You can always go back and delete the file when you complete your scrapbook page.

Using WordArt

Another way to create unique and original titles for your scrapbook pages is to use the WordArt feature, found as a slanted A icon usually on the toolbar for your drawing features. (An icon is a small image or graphic that represents a software program, a capability, a task within a program, or some kind of shortcut to an application.)

3 | The new font isn't the same size as the other, so I enlarged it to create a title that would be more bold.

1 On the bottom of the screen you'll see the tool bar and the slanted A icon for WordArt.

2 Click on the slanted A and you will see a gallery of templates on the screen.

3 After selecting a template, a new box will open on your screen that allows you to type in your text.

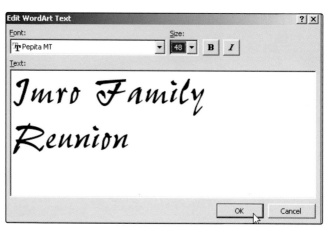

4 Select a font and size, then type in your text and click on the OK button. Note it looks like the title is done on two lines, but the finished WordArt will be one line of text.

5 Clicking OK lets the program insert your WordArt title onto a blank page. After you print the page, you can finish creating the page with your photos, captions, and journaling.

This page's title and journaling were printed on a separate acetate sheet.

FROM PROCESSING TO PAGES

Creating a title in your word processing program may be your first step or last step in designing a scrapbook page. You may want to print your title on decorative or colored paper and fill in the rest with more traditional scrapbook elements like die cuts, stickers, eyelets, brads, and charms. Or add something interesting like lace, ribbon, raffia, buttons, or dried floral elements. You can use all your decorative punches and scissors. And don't forget your photos!

The idea of using a word processing program is to take the stress out of having to perfectly handwrite every title, caption, or journaling. Enjoy the ability to use decorative and specialty fonts in your titles. You may want to stick to simpler, easy-to-read fonts for your captions and journaling, so have some fun with your titles. Word processing lets you add a touch of soft color or a blast of bold color without the messiness of ink pens and markers. Titles printed using today's printers don't easily splotch or smear. (Be aware that photo-quality printers printing on photo-quality paper are still sensitive to smudging until completely dry. You'll learn more about printing and printers on page 94.)

I've only covered some of the basic ways to use word processing for scrapbooking in this section. To find out more of your software's capabilities, take some time to read the owner's manual, a how-to book, or use the software's Help section. Usually there is a condensed set of notes that gives you an understanding of the most commonly used features and different shortcuts built into the program.

Reading a manual isn't fun and can seem like a waste of time, but it's time well spent to expand your creativity. Some programs even contain tutorials and help functions, which show how to use each feature of the program. Most of all I encourage you to have fun as you experiment.

You can also use word processing programs to create totally digital layouts. You can create a title, insert a photograph or two, and complete the page with captions or journaling. To learn how to import graphics or photos into word processing, see page 127; and to know more about finding and importing clip art, see page 111. Besides photos, you can insert clip art, borders, and other graphics to give you even more design capabilities.

A totally digital page can be viewed electronically on your computer screen, sent as a special surprise in an e-mail, placed into a digital scrapbook, sent on a CD, uploaded onto a website or mail list, or printed out on plain or decorative acid-free paper. You'll learn how to create an entire digital scrapbook page later in the book. (See page 127.)

FONT FEVER

There is a font for every mood, emotion, theme, and motif—versatile creative elements like this are perfect for scrapbook design. Fonts can be simple or intricate. You can mix and match fonts to create continuity on a page or throughout a scrapbook. In fact, finding and using new fonts can become quite addictive!

Beyond the fonts in your word processing program, you can add unique fonts by purchasing font software or downloading font freeware or shareware from the Internet. Freeware is any type of software that is offered free, whereas with shareware there is an understood agreement that if you like the software you will pay for its use to the shareware creator. Many free fonts are available on the Web—to learn more about finding, downloading, and applying these fonts, look under Finding Free Fonts on page 108.

A font (also called type) is a set or group of printable and displayable text characters in a specific style and size. The type design for a set of fonts is known as the typeface and variations on the design form the typeface family. For example:

Arial is a typeface family
Arial italic is a typeface
Arial italic 10-point is a font

A font is either serif, which has fine lines or finishing strokes on each letter, or sans serif, which is without decorative finishing strokes. Serif lettering is more formal or elaborate, while sans serif is more casual or modern looking.

Classic rules-of-thumb for designing with fonts are to use no more than two different fonts within a design, such as a scrapbook page. Also, do not mix serif with sans serif type on the same page, although there are rare exceptions when this can be done.

You can find the fonts available to you in your word processing program. You usually have a good variety that comes with the original software, and you can always add more fonts.

To use your font options, you'll find the font window in your word processing program. You can select a font as well as a size, known as point size, for the font.

Adding More Fonts

You can add more fonts to your word processing program by purchasing fonts as a software package. Most font software comes with hundreds or thousands of fonts. Be sure to check the system requirements before purchasing font software. To install, insert the CD or diskette into your computer, and follow the instructions on the screen. (See page 32.)

Deleting Fonts

You may only like and use a handful of the fonts within the software package. It's easy to delete fonts that you don't use or like.

Click to open your Control Panel, then open the Fonts Folder.

With and Without

Here's a list of a few fonts that are either serif or sans serif:

SERIF	SANS SERIF
Arrus	Arial Narrow
Bernhard Modern	Arquitectura
Centinneal	Bernhard Tango
Ellington	Bisque
Garamond	Charlotte Sans
Playbill	Franklin Gothic
Times New Roman	Gill Sans MT
Typewriter	Papyrus

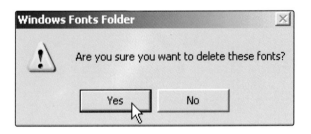

2 Locate the unwanted font and select or highlight it. Click on the File button at the top of the screen. Select Delete option.

3 A screen box will ask you whether you really want to delete the item. Click Yes and the font is deleted.

Fonts as Templates

Many scrapbookers use unique and specialty fonts as templates. Instead of printing, trimming, matting, and adhering the title, you can print out the font, then trace the letters unto a page. From there, you can use markers or colored pencils to bring the title to life.

Begin by printing a title for a scrapbook page using a specialty font.

Using a light box or window with full sun, trace the font onto your background page or plain paper. Get as creative as you like by using colored pencils, markers, or pens to complete the title design. If you traced directly onto your background paper, you are now ready to fill up the page with photos and captions. If you traced the decorative font onto plain paper, you can trim and mat the title and adhere it onto the page with the rest of your page elements.

If you don't have a light box or don't want to trace a font, you can still benefit from having specialty fonts on your computer. Just find the font you want to use, type your title or journaling, and highlight the text.

Highlight the text on the screen.

Select a light color, such as pale yellow, light blue, or gray for coloring the font. By choosing a light color, you'll find it's easier to go over the letters with darker colored pencils, pens, or markers if desired. If you don't have a color printer, the light colors will print in light gray, providing you with an outline for adding your own touches. A final option is to print the specialty font in the main color you wish to use, then color in the background or open areas as desired.

Printing specialty fonts in light colors allows you to use pens, pencils, or markers in darker colors to create the effects you want.

A final option is to color print the specialty font in the main color you wish to use, and then color in the background or open areas.

JOURNALING SOFTWARE

Word processing adds to your creativity skills, but it has its own limits. Sometimes it would just be fun to have your journaling words float up and down or swirl around the page, but if you're like me, my artistic flair is cut short by my lack of artistic discipline. In other words, I'm in a hurry and want it without all the work. Journaling software, like Journaling Genie, shown here, can provide these for you. I use Journaling Genie, which allows you to type in text as a title, caption, or journaling, and converts the text into swirls, curls, and other artistic shapes with a click of your mouse.

Creating Lines of Text

Begin by installing the journaling software. (See page 32 for installing software.)

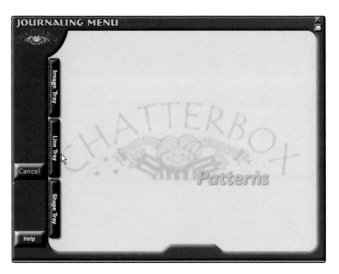

1 Open the software. Click on New. This will open a new screen that gives you some choices. You can select to use an Image (clip art), Line (for lines of text), or Shape (text converted into a shape).

2 Select Image, Line, or Shape. For this example, Line (as in a line of text) was selected. You can now select what line you want for your text, either

for a title, caption, or journaling, to follow. Click on the line shape you want. This example clicked on the first line shape called Curls.

3 Click on the Create button, and a new screen will appear with the selected line.

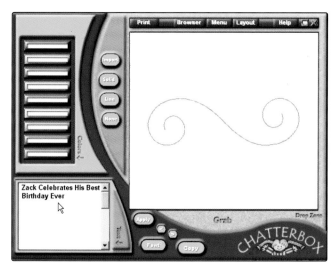

4 Type in your text, then click the Apply button and, like magic, you will have your formatted text.

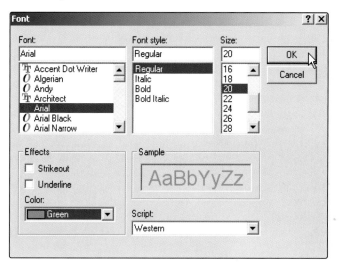

5 The default font in this program, CB Brush Strokes, was difficult to read in the chosen line shape.

6 To select an easier font to read, like Arial, click on Font. The font screen box that appears gives you the ability to change the font, select a font style, and font size. You also have some style choices like Underline and Color. The sample box shows you how the font will look. After you are satisfied with the changes, click the OK button.

7 You can print the results to cut and mat on a page. Or, you can move the line where you want it on the paper before printing, allowing you to design a title and place it on your page.

Text Shapes

Like a text box in your word processing program, the journaling program provides you with a variety of shapes.

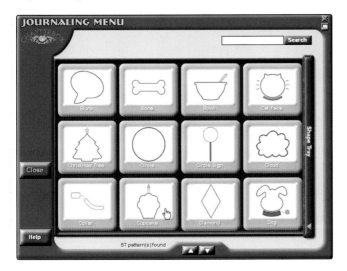

Open the software. Select New, then Create, then Shape. There are plenty of shapes to choose from in this program. Follow the same process of typing in text and making adjustments for the font and styles as you did for the line text. Let's try the Cupcake.

2 Select Cupcake and click Create. Type in your text, click Apply, and it's ready to print.

The finished page makes a lasting memory of a special day.

Friends

This simple use of fonts creates a handsome page that says it all. The variations are end-less—and you will always have the last word.

MATERIALS

Photo
2 coordinating decorative papers
2 sheets of acid-free paper in a color of your choice
Background paper
Metal letters suitable for grommeting
Grommets

SOFTWARE & TOOLS

Word-processing software
Decorative fonts
Scissors or paper trimmer
Acid-free adhesive
Grommet tool

Designers: Maria Nerius & Terry Taylor

INSTRUCTIONS

1. The photo used for this project was a digital image. If you need to, bring your photo into your photo-editing program and resize. Print and trim the photo. Double mat with coordinating papers. For a different look, you can double mat only the corners as shown.

2. Open your word-processing software. Find Page Setup under the File menu. Open the Page Setup and change all your margins—top, bottom, left, and right—to .5, since you want to use as much of the page as possible.

3. Type the word Friends at the top and the words, You & Me at the bottom. You may have to adjust this as you continue to design the page. I usu-ally begin with this basic structure using my default font (Times New Roman) in 18-to 20-point size.

4. Fill the page with words as shown. Highlight each word and change the font. You can vary the font size, use different colors, boldface, and italicize.

5. Adjust the title size to fit. When you are happy with the font design, print 2 copies on the colored paper.

6. Position the photo on the background paper, and adhere. Cut one of the font sheets to accommodate the title and journaling, and adhere. Cut the other font sheet into seven squares that, when evenly spaced, will run down the right side of the page, and adhere.

7. Attach the metal letters with grommets using the grommet tool.

Reading List

This simple design is a fun and easy way to keep track of accomplishments at school. In years to come, you and your child will enjoy looking over the first-grade reading list. The addition of the bookmarks is a handy way to include art memorabilia.

MATERIALS

Memorabilia

SOFTWARE & TOOLS

Word-processing
  software
Fonts
Acid-free adhesive

Designer: Susan McBride

INSTRUCTIONS

1. In your word-processing program, use Page Setup, to create two 8½ x 11-inch (21.3 x 27.5 cm) pages. Set your margins as far out as possible to accommodate your printer.

2. Fonts used for this design were chosen for their nostalgic classroom feel. The typewriter font is called Date Line. The handwritten, chalkboard type is called Eraser Dust. The little people were created using a font called Minipicks.

3. Create your pages. Create a full-page text box with a black border, and fill the box with a color resembling chalkboard green. Choose white for your font color, and create the page using the fonts selected. For the first page, the designer mixed the fonts when listing the books—the numbers appear to be handwritten, and the text looks to be typewritten. She underlined the text to give a primary school feel to this simple design.

4. For the next page, allow blank space for displaying the bookmarks made by the children during the school year. Use the same fonts to repeat the motif.

5. Print, then use acid-free adhesive to adhere the bookmarks.

Take a Letter, Lizzy

Finding a unique font to use for journaling, page title, or captions can help highlight the theme of a scrapbook page. To go with the photo, I used an old-fashioned typewriter font for the journaled letter. Finding the right rubber stamp allowed me to create a way to pull the finished page from the typewriter!

MATERIALS

Typewriter rubber stamp
2 pieces of glossy white cardstock
Silver metallic cardstock
Glossy black cardstock
Photo
Typewriter rubber stamp alphabet set
Acid-free white paper

SOFTWARE & TOOLS

Watercolor black dye inkpad
Craft knife and cutting pad
Scissors
Acid-free adhesive
Computer
Ink-jet printer
Word processing/journaling software
Typewriter font

Designer: Maria Nerius

INSTRUCTIONS

1. Stamp the typewriter image onto the glossy white cardstock. Trim as necessary. Using your craft knife, cut a slot across the top of the stamped typewriter to correspond with the positioning of the paper in a real typewriter.

2. Mat the typewriter image onto the silver metallic paper, trimming as necessary. Make sure not to glue the slot closed or to glue the area under the slot–you want this to remain free to allow you to slide your journaling in later on. Trim. Double mat onto glossy black cardstock, and trim.

3. Crop the photo as needed. In this layout, I enlarged the original photo via scanning. The original photo had deckled edges and a stamped date. Since I wanted to keep the date, I cropped the photo on three sides. Once I printed the photo, I used plain scissors to create a new deckled edge–you can also use decorative-edge scissors to get a similar effect. Mat the photo on the silver paper, then on the black paper, as you did for the typewriter.

4. Position the matted photo and typewriter image onto glossy white cardstock to determine where you'll rubber-stamp the alphabet. Do not adhere either the photo or the typewriter image at this point.

5. If you have never worked with glossy cardstock, be aware that it has a very slick surface. Ink your stamp, and then lightly but firmly press down on the stamp. Lift straight up without shaking or wiggling the stamp. Shaking or wiggling the stamp will cause the image to smear. You may want to practice on a scrap of glossy paper first.

6. Stamp your alphabet letters in the determined positions–to the right side of the photo and to the left side of the typewriter image. Once the ink dries, adhere the photo and typewriter image to the background paper.

7. Measure the width of the slot you cut on the typewriter image. Cut a piece of silver metallic paper slightly narrower than this width and at least 1 inch (2.5 cm) longer than the height of the typewriter image. Insert the cut piece of silver paper into the slot to make sure it slides easily.

8. Using your word-processing program with the typewriter font, type out your journaling message. Use a small point size, such as 10 or 12. You may have to try a few point sizes to make sure the journaling will fit onto the silver mat. Trim the journaling and adhere to the silver mat. Slide into typewriter.

SCANNING

Scanning gives you unlimited creativity for scrap-booking. You can compose a whole scrapbook page on the scanner bed, or scan objects for a custom background paper. The practical side of scanning is that it allows you to easily import all kinds of photos and images into your computer.

GIVE IT A TRY

You can lay both flat and dimensional objects on the bed for scanning. After closing the lid, you click for a pre-scan, which allows you to see the image on your computer screen. At this time, you can make any adjustments to the items to be scanned. You'll complete another pre-scan, and if you are happy with the result you'll click for a true scan. The true scan can then be printed, sent by e-mail, or saved.

Scanners give you several options on how the saved scan can be saved. You can save as a JPEG, TIFF, and several other digital options. If you save as a JPEG you will also have an additional screen box that lets you select how condensed or of what quality you want the JPEG to be. The higher the quality, the bigger the file will be. You might want medium to low quality for a Web page, while you want medium to high quality for an e-mail if you think the recipient will be printing the images.

Try scanning the following items to see how versatile your scanner can be. You might also want to save some of your scans to get a handle on how to save images. Try creating a folder to hold your saved images/files. This exercise will help you get a good start on keeping your digital elements organized on your computer. Experiment and have some fun scanning different items. The more you use your scanner, the easier it becomes to expand your creativity.

- A photo
- A map
- A stone or a few pebbles
- A leaf
- A fresh flower
- Your hand
- A scrapbook page
- A lace tablecloth

OUTPUT RESOLUTION

The scanner has software that gives you a wide range of options. An important option is *output resolution*. Resolution with the scanner is measured in dpi (dots per inch). The higher the resolution, the more detail you will have when you print the graphic or text. Just like TIFF and JPEG, you will select low (100 or 200) or high (300, 600, or 1200) resolution to coordinate with how you will use your scanned image. A drawn image, photograph, or document looks better when printed out with a resolution of 300 to 600 dpi. Whereas, if you only want to use the image for electronic viewing, you can scan it at 200 dpi and it will look great in an e-mail or on a Web page. Keep in mind that the higher the resolution or dpi, the more memory you will need to store or save it.

A pull down menu allows you to easily change the selection of your output resolution.

OUTPUT TYPE

Another option on your scanner deals with the *output type*. You'll have several selections including True Color, Grayscale, Black and White (bitmap/raster or scalable/vector), 256 Color (Web, system, or optimized palette), Spot Color, Text, and Text and Image. For your scrapbooking you will mainly be using *true color* and *grayscale*. True color can be thought of as real color, meaning that the colors within your scan or printed scan, will pretty much match the color of the original.

Grayscale can be interchanged with what most of us call black and white. You can experiment with the black-and-white output, but this isn't the best option for most photographs or graphics you'll want to use in your scrapbooking, because this black-and-white feature is used for electronic applications.

For Web and simple graphics, designers use the 256-color palette or Bit Mapped format (.bmp). While this limits the number of colors you can use, it speeds up downloads. However, for most of your digital scrapbooking, stick with true color; it is easy to use and produces better results. If you end up becoming a Website designer after reading this book, then you'll have a chance to use the 256-color output type on your scanner.

You can experiment with your output selections. Scan anything that has full color, like a photograph or a flower with a stem and leaves. Go to your output type options (this feature usually is in the toolbar that runs across the top of the screen box) in the scanner, and click on grayscale. You should see the graphic as a black and white image rather than color. Go ahead and click other options like black-and-white or spot color. If you click print, the scan will print as the option you selected. Even a color printer will print out a grayscale image if that is the output type you selected.

Examples of a scanned full-color image, top, and of grayscale output, below

EDITING ON THE SCANNER

Most scanner software gives you some editing capabilities. You can crop a scanned item like a photograph. This option comes in handy by allowing you to crop a photo or graphic to your liking before saving the image. You can't correct red-eye, insert text, or restore part of an image with a scanner—you'll need your photo-editing software for those situations.

1 Open the scanner and lay the photo on the scanner bed. Pre-scan the photo. Then select the area to scan. This is like cropping the photo before you scan it, without permanently altering the original photo.

JPEG Options

2 Click to save. If you are saving as a JPEG image, you'll be asked how much you want to compress it. Low is OK for sending as an electronic image, while high is better for print quality. Select and click OK.

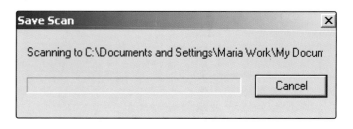

3 You'll get a screen box telling you that scanning is taking place

4 The result is a cropped scanned image saved as a JPEG.

Remember Copyright Rules

Please keep in mind that although scanning isn't exactly like using a copier machine, the process is similar, and you need to be aware that copyright laws protect many patterned or decorative scrapbook papers. You can't just scan your favorite decorative pages and print out a dozen or so. The same goes for copyrighted stickers, die cuts, and clip art.

Most manufacturers will list what can or can't be done with their copyrighted materials. There are many manufacturers who publish copyright and royalty-free materials, meaning you can copy and manipulate those graphics as much as you want.

Arranging the items on the scanner bed created a page ready for the photo.

SLIDES AND TRANSPARENCIES TO PHOTOS

Get out all those old slides and photo transparencies. This time you won't need to set up the projector and screen to enjoy those wonderful memories. All you need is your scanner and the slide/transparency adapter, which is a light fixture that plugs into the back of your scanner. Two black plastic holder sheets are also included. One will hold your slides, and the other will hold transparencies while the scanner does its job. This adapter system can also be referred to as an Active Transparency Adapter (XPA).

To use it, you first place your slides (usually up to four) into the openings of the plastic holder sheet. Place this sheet on your scanner bed. Then you place the adapter light on top of the slides/holder. Most scanners come with this adapter, and many new scanners come with the adapter built into the scanner's lid. If your scanner doesn't have an adapter, you can purchase one separately.

Transparencies are handled the exact same way as slides, except that the plastic holder is designed with either a larger opening for big transparencies (older photo negatives) or two slots to better hold a strip of transparencies (more modern film negatives).

TRANSFORMING THE SLIDE

Plug in the slide/transparency adapter for your scanner. Please be aware that this adapter puts out light even when you are not scanning. The light does heat up the scanning area, so never leave any slides or negative in the adapter unattended. Even five minutes can cause the slide or transparency to curl.

Open your scanner software. You need to make sure the Transparency Exposure Adjustment feature under the Tool options is on. You will need a resolution output of 300 to 600 dpi for saving the image as a JPEG for electronic viewing. You must have a resolution output of 600 to 1200 dpi if you want to print the image. Your scanner may give you a message that the resolution doesn't need to be set so high, but ignore it! You need the resolution to get a clear, crisp image for printing.

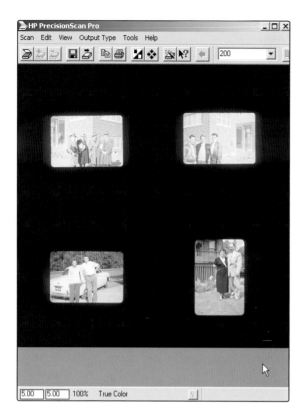

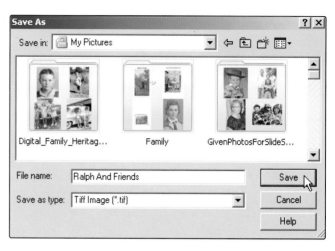

Click Save As and type in your file name. Select the format for saving the image. Select JPEG for an electronically viewed image or TIFF for an image you will print. Make sure you place the image in a folder you can find!

1 Lay slides with the front (usually marked with a film company name) side down into the plastic slide holder sheet. Place the adapter unit on top of the slide holder. Pre-scan image.

4 Open the image file in photo-editing software, and edit if you wish. Then your image is ready to print.

2 Select the area to scan. The images will appear rather dark until you select the area. Once you've selected an area, you will see a better, cleaner image.

Ski Trip

This scrapbook page begins with a simple flat scan of a regional map that becomes the decorative background paper. By adding your photo, memorabilia, and extra embellishments, you can easily create a lasting memory for a wonderful trip.

Maria Nerius

MATERIALS

Regional map
2 sheets of yellow acid-free paper
Ski trail map
Photos
1 sheet of blue acid-free paper
Memorabilia
Embellishments

SOFTWARE & TOOLS

Scanner
Scissors or personal trimmer
Acid-free adhesive

INSTRUCTIONS

1. Scan the regional map at 200 dpi and save as a JPEG or TIFF. Open the map file in your photo-editing program, and print. Trim the map as needed, and adhere itto one sheet of the yellow paper.

2. Fold the ski trail map so that it will open showing only the ski trails.

3. Cut a rectangular piece of the yellow paper so it is slightly larger than the folded trail map. Adhere this paper to the top of the folded trail map. Adhere the back of the folded trail map to the background paper.

4. Crop your photos, and mat them on the blue paper. Adhere one photo near the top of the front of the trail map. Adhere the memorabilia to the bottom of the front.

5. Open the trail map, and adhere the second photo to the map. If desired, attach embellishments.

   Note: You can adapt this design using any map or trail guide. Brochures and maps from museums or historical sites also work well.

Backyard Backgrounds

You can scan dimensional objects! Take a piece of your own backyard, and turn it into unique background papers by using filters in your photo-editing program. Where your filters (see page 54) are located and how each is named can vary from one photo-editing program to another.

Designer: Maria Nerius

MATERIALS

Flower, leaf, branch, or twig
Mirror paper in gold
2 to 4 coordinating acid-free papers
Photos
Brass word plate
Bright white paper for inkjet printers
White cardstock or heavyweight paper
Brad

SOFTWARE & TOOLS

Scanner
Photo-editing software
Printer
Scissors or personal trimmer
Acid-free adhesive
Eyelet setter
Acid-free marker or pen

Daydreaming

1. Scan a branch at 200 dpi, and save as a JPEG or a TIFF file. Open the file in your photo-editing software, then print the image.

2. Find and click the Filter button in your software. Select the Texture filter, then apply the filter. A texture filter creates a tiny variation in your original image that gives the illusion of texture. It also gives an instant aged look to an image.

3. Print the filtered image. If you want to use the altered image in the future, remember to save the filtered image as a separate JPEG or TIFF.

4. Note the horizontal layout of the page. Trim the filtered image to 10 x 7 ¼ inches (25 x 18.1 cm) and adhere to 10 ¼ x 7 ½-inch (26.25 x 18.75 cm) gold mirror paper. Adhere this to the black background paper, positioning the matted image slightly above center to allow for gluing the brass word plate at the bottom.

5. Crop the photo and mat to gold mirror paper. Then mat the matted photo to black paper to make a double mat. Adhere the matted photo on a slight diagonal to the center of the page.

6. Glue the brass word plate to the bottom center of the page.

Designer: Maria Nerius

Kaleidoscope

1. Scan a branch at 200 dpi, and save as a JPEG or a TIFF file. Open the file in your photo-editing software, then print the image.

2. Find and click the Kaleidoscope button in your software. Select the Kaleidoscope filter, then apply the filter. A kaleidoscope filter turns your image into a fascinating kaleidoscope pattern that totally obscures the original image.

3. Print two filtered images. Print the first image on bright white paper and the second image on white cardstock. If you want to use the altered image in the future, remember to save the filtered image as a JPEG or TIFF.

4. Trim the image printed on bright white paper to 7¼ x 10 inches (18.1 x 25cm) and adhere to a solid background paper.

5. Cut out the center of the second filter image that is printed on cardstock—it almost looks like a flower once it's cut out.

6. Line up the cut cardstock image to the image you adhered to the background paper. With the tip of your scissors, make a small hole through both. Insert a brad into the hole, and flatten the tongs at the back of the page.

7. Crop your photo. Make sure your photo is smaller than the cutout kaleidoscope image, since you want to avoid seeing the photo until you turn the top. Adhere the photo to the background paper.

This Old House

If you have old photos taken with an instant camera, you know how quickly they age. By scanning those fading photos, you can create renewed images that will weather the test of time.

MATERIALS

Instant-film photos
Solid-color acid-free
  papers
Photo paper

SOFTWARE & TOOLS

Scanner
Printer
Photo-editing software
Scissors or paper trimmer
Adhesive

INSTRUCTIONS

1. The background paper for this project was created by taking a digital photo of the home's brick exterior. Walk around your home and see if you can find any interesting textures that you can photograph to create your own background paper.

Designers: Maria Nerius & Terry Taylor

2. Bring the image into your computer. If you don't have a digital camera, take the picture and bring it into your computer using one of the options found on page 38. Print two images on glossy photo paper. To make the pages 12 x 12-inches (30 x 30 cm), adhere them onto 12 x 12-inch pages. If preferred, you can also keep the pages 8½ x 11-inches (21.3 x 27.5 cm).

3. Scan your instant-film photos, and save as a high-resolution JPEG or in TIFF format. Open the scanned photos in your photo-editing software. Crop if needed. Use auto enhance to lighten any dark photos. Over time, many instant-film photos not only fade, but darken. By using your photo-enhancing options, you can make the photos much clearer.

4. Print the scanned photos, trim as needed, and mat them. The two papers used for matting were woodgrain and grass background papers.

5. Use the woodgrain paper to create the workman's sign and labels for your lettering. The letters used here are press-on letters; however, you can create title or journaling using your word-processing software.

6. Adhere the photos. Since this is a two-page spread, place the title on the left-hand page. Embellish with press-on images of tools as desired.

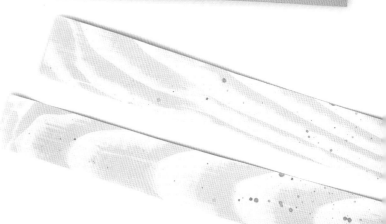

USING PHOTO-EDITING SOFTWARE WITH SCANNED IMAGES

Once scanned images are in your computer, there are many options for changing those images to your liking. The following seven projects combine scanning with the use of a photo-editing program.

If you do not have the photo-editing software used to create these projects, explore the program you do have for similar features.

Celtic Border

Designer: Shannon Yokeley

You can change the color of clip art to your liking. Many programs have a paint or fill feature that allows you add colors at the click of a mouse. Once you get a design you like, experiment with using different color combinations.

MATERIALS

Clip art

SOFTWARE & TOOLS

Flatbed Scanner with scanning software
Adobe PhotoShop

INSTRUCTIONS

1. Scan in the clipart you selected at 300 dpi at the percentage you need to fill the page to your liking.

2. To make the images as black and white as possible, go to the Image menu, then the Levels menus, then to the adjust tab. Pull the two end tabs slowly together until the white is pure white and the black is pure black.

3. To sharpen the image as needed, go to the Filters menu and at the Sharpen tab select Unsharp Mask. Adjust the levels in this menu until you are satisfied.

4. To add color to the black-and-white image, use the Paint Bucket tool and select the first color. Click in the white space you wish to fill with color. Repeat this process until the whole image is colored. Save the image as a TIFF, and print out.

Children's Page

A layer in a photo-editing program is much like creating an overlay on a scrapbook page using acetate or vellum. The layers used here add color to the clip art images.

MATERIALS
Clip art

SOFTWARE & TOOLS
Flatbed Scanner with scanning software
Adobe PhotoShop software

INSTRUCTIONS

1. Scan the clipart you at 300 dpi at the percentage needed.

2. To make the image as black and white as possible, go to the the Image menu, then to the Levels menu, then to the Adjust tab. Pull the two end tabs slowly together until the white is pure white and the black is pure black.

3. To sharpen the image, go to the Filters menu and at the Sharpen tab select Unsharp Mask. Adjust the levels in this menu until you are satisfied.

4. To add color to the black-and-white image, first go to the Layers Palette to create a new layer and set the blending mode at Screen. The new colors will overlay the black of the drawing.allowing the white to remain white.

5. Select your color. Using the Brush tool, place the color whre you want it. You can always erase any mistakes you make. Continue selecting and applying new colors until the clip art is painted to your liking.

Designer: Shannon Yokeley

6. Before adding the color blocks behind the clipart, you have to flatten the image, which makes two layers one image. From the Layer menu, scroll down to Flatten Image and select it. Note: you won't be able to separate the layers once you flatten them.

7. To add the color blocks, select your first color. with the Rectangular Marquee tool, select the area to be colored. With the Paint Bucket tool, click on the selected area. Since the color will be applied to only uninterrupted white space, you may have go back and fill areas with color as needed. Keep repeating this process for any color blocks you wish to make.

8. To preserve the colors you've already done, make sure to deselect an area before selecting the next area you work on. Repeat steps 7 and 8 for the remaining areas. Save as a TIFF, and print out.

A Field of Daisies

Designer: Shannon Yokeley

At first glance, it looks as if you would have to lay a fortune in fabric daises on the scanner bed to get this page. But it only took three daises to generate this field of flowers using the principle of cut and paste.

MATERIALS

Several fabric daisies

SOFTWARE & TOOLS

Flatbed Scanner with scanning software
Adobe PhotoShop software

INSTRUCTIONS

1. Place several fabric daisies on the scanner. Scan them at 300 dpi at 100 percent. Bring the scanned image into the photo-editing program. Change the canvas size to 8½ x 11 inches (21.3 x 27.5 cm) by going to the Image menu and then to Canvas Size.

2. Use the Eraser tool to get a clean background. Using the Marquee tool, select one daisy. With the Move tool, move the daisy to the beginning of your pattern. Do this to each of the daisies you scanned.

3. Using the Marquee tool, select one of the daisies, then use copy and paste to add another daisy to the pattern. Since this adds another layer to the image, move the new daisy to its correct place before repeating.

4. Once you have completed the pattern, flatten the image to make one layer. Go to the Layer menu and select Flatten image.

5. For minor color correcting, go to the Image menu, then the Adjust tab which will take you to Variations. Select and add the colors needed to correct.

6. If the image needs sharpening, go to the Filters menu. At the Sharpen tab select Unsharp Mask. Adjust the levels in this menu until you are satisfied. Be careful not to over-sharpen the image. If you do, the edges of the objects will start to get a halo effect around them. Save the image as a TIFF, and print out.

Drawing Page

Although the page looks as if it were composed on the scanner bed, it actually merges two separate image files. The shadows added to the art supplies give them a three-dimensional look.

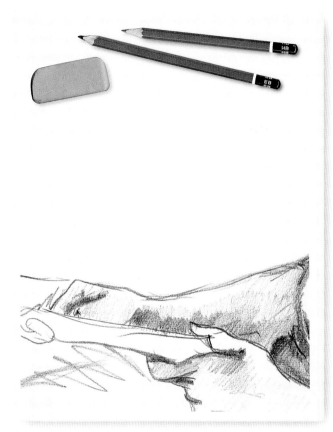

MATERIALS

Art supplies
Drawing made on white paper

SOFTWARE & TOOLS

Flatbed Scanner with scanning software
Adobe PhotoShop software

Designer: Shannon Yokeley

INSTRUCTIONS

1. Scan the drawing at 300 dpi and 100 percent, then open the image in PhotoShop. Using the eraser tool, clean up the drawing. If your scanned image is not already 8½ x 11 inches (21.3 x 27.5 cm), go the Image menu, then to Canvas Size to change the measurements.

2. Scan the art supplies in another document. Arrange themon the scanner bed as you want them to appear, then preview the image. If needed, rearrange and preview until you are ready for the final scan.

3. Once you've scanned the art supplies, open the file in the photo-editing program. Clean up the image by using the eraser tool. Use the Magic Wand tool to select the white background. This allows you to draw on the image. Using the Airbrush tool, select a dark gray color and draw in the shadows. If needed, you can use the Eraser tool to erase any mistakes.

4. Select the image of the art supplies. From the Edit menu select Copy. Go to the scan of the drawing and from the Edit menu select Paste. You now have two layers in the image, With the Move tool, move the new layer (the art supplies) around the page until you are satisfied.

5. Make the layers one. From the Layer menu, scroll down to Flatten Image and select it. Save the image as a Tiff, and print out.

Journaling Page

This page provides a beautiful space for journaling and gives you ample room to include names, dates, and remembrances.

MATERIALS

Clip art

SOFTWARE & TOOLS

Flatbed Scanner with scanning software
Adobe PhotoShop software

INSTRUCTIONS

1. Scan your selected clip art at 300 dpi at the percentage you need to fill the page to your liking.

2. To make the image as pure black and white as possible, go to the Image menu, then the Levels menu, then to the Adjust tab. Pull the two ends tabs slowly together until the white is pure white and the black is pure black.

3. To sharpen the image as needed, go to the Filters menu and at the Sharpen tab select Unsharp Mask. Adjsut the levels in this menu until you are satisfied.

4. From the Layers Palette, create a new layer and set the blending mode at Screen. The new colors will overlay the black of the drawing while allowing the white to remain white.

5. Select a color for drawing. Using the Rectangular Marquee tool, draw a box around the clip art. Using the Paint Bucket tool, repeat this step until the image is colored to your satisfaction.

6. Before adding the color blocks behind the now clipart, you have to flatten the image.

Designer: Shannon Yokeley

From the Layer menu, scroll down to Flatten Image and select it. Note: you won't be able to separate the layers once you flatten them

7. To add the color blocks, select your first color. block. With the Rectangular Marquee tool, select the area to be colored.Using the Paint Bucket tool, click in the selected area. Keep repeating this step for all color blocks. To get the blocks perfectly aligned, pull the guidelines from the rulers.

8. Select a color for the journaling lines. Select the line tool and set the point size for the line, to determine it's thickness. To keep the line perfeclty straight, hold down the shift key before starting to draw, otherwise you will draw a curved line. Draw the lines where needed. Save the image as a TIFF, and print.

Floral Page with Oval Template

Create your own template on a scanned image without using scissors and glue. By fading a selected area, you can create a perfect frame for your photos. The floral background is made by scanning silk flowers then blurring them for a softer look.

MATERIALS

Silk flowers

SOFTWARE & TOOLS

Flatbed Scanner with scanning software
Adobe PhotoShop software

INSTRUCTIONS

1. Place silk flowers on the scanner bed. Set the resolution at 300 dpi and 100 percent. Preview before doing the final scan. If you are not happy with the preview, rearrange the silk flowers and preview until satisfied.

2. Open the image in your photo-editing program. If you need to do some minor color correcting, go to the Image menu, then the Adjust tab that will take you to Variations. Select and add the colors needed for correction.

3. Now go to the Filter menu and scroll down to the Blur tab and select Smart Blur. In this palette select the adjustments that give you the results you like best.

4. To add the oval in the image, use the Elliptical Marquee tool to select the area you wish to fade back. With this area still selected, go to the Image menu to the Adjust tab and select Levels. You will see Output Levels on the

Designer: Shannon Yokeley

bottom of the palette. On the bar below click and hold down the black triangle on the left and slide the triangle to the right slowly. You will notice the oval start to lighten, keep sliding the triangle until you are satisfied with the results. Save it as a TIFF, and print out.

PRINTING

A computer system without a printer is like a peanut butter and jelly sandwich without the bread. Your printer is the component that will allow you to take a digital image that can only be viewed electronically and print out an image you can use for your scrapbook pages. Whether you print text for titles or captions, print graphics for borders or frames, or print photos, your printer is the final electronic step before creating your traditional scrapbook pages.

PRINT IT!

The type of printer used for most scrapbooking is a color ink-jet printer. Its moderate price and easy use make it a must for most of us. The other type of printer is called a laser printer. Laser printers are more commonly used for high-speed printing of reports and documents, and do not provide the color range needed for scrapbooking. If you're lucky enough to have both types of printers, you may want to use your laser printer for journaling or other heavy text memory crafting.

If you're serious about printing your own photography, or using your scanner to make prints from originals, you may want to consider a color ink-jet printer that is specifically designed for printing photos. This style of printer is usually called a photo-quality ink-jet and is a great investment for the serious scrapbooker. You'll find many choices on the market. A photo-quality printer will give you more printing options and make better quality photo prints. This type of printer can also handle just about any type of paper you want to use, from heavy to lightweight. The most expensive aspect of the color ink-jet printer is not the printer itself, but the ink cartridges used by the printer and the photo paper used to print high-quality photos. I recommend selecting a printer that has separate cartridges for black and color inks, rather than an all-in-one cartridge. In the long run, separate cartridges will save you money because, with normal use, you will use more color inks than black inks when printing photographs.

When printing anything, you will usually want to print a test copy. The test copy lets you check the overall quality of the print. The test copy should be done with black ink and plain computer paper. If you make any adjustments to the print (text, graphic, or photograph), it's always best to run another test copy before using full color and your quality paper.

PAPER

For most of us creative types, the most exciting accessory is the multitude of papers available for printing our photographic masterpieces and scrapbook elements. You can always use the standard bright white computer paper, but for projects and

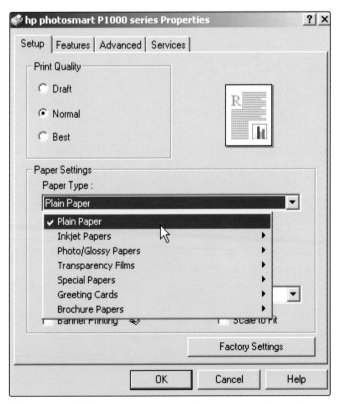

This printer's Properties screen allows you to select the type of paper you'll be using, gives you a selection of black or colored ink, and lets you know when your ink is running low.

added scrapbook creativity you'll want to include some glossy and matte photo paper, canvas or textured paper, decorative background papers, label paper, greeting card paper, and even some decal or "shrink art" paper.

Today's printers are very sophisticated and in some ways very sensitive to the different types of papers you select to use in your scrapbooking. Most printers allow you to select the type of paper you are printing on. One very important item when printing is being aware of your printer's options menus before hitting the final print button. You can select the amount of ink used, the quality of the print, and the speed of the print.

Most papers will come with some indication of what printer settings you need to use. For example, when using fabric papers (fabric that has a removable paper backing), the manufacturer tells you to use the plain paper setting. This setting uses less ink, and that's important to the success of your final printed fabric paper. Too much ink and the design or photo will not have a crisp image.

Know Your Paper

The following descriptions of various papers should help you when deciding what paper to use for your scrapbook printing projects.

Plain paper is lightweight, inexpensive paper used for most printer uses when color is not important. This is also the paper you will use when doing print tests.

Bright white paper, which is slightly more expensive than plain paper, is lightweight paper that is designed specifically for color copying since it really shows off color.

Photo-quality paper can be lightweight or heavyweight. It has a coated finish designed specifically for printing photographs. This type of

paper has a right and wrong side. You'll find that there is a great variety of photo paper available, but keep in mind that some ink-jet printers cannot handle the heavyweight or specialty papers.

Glossy photograph paper has a very slick or shiny finish that is the right side for printing. When using glossy photo paper, it is best to use the same brand as your printer. Most printer manufacturers offer their own brand of glossy and photo-quality paper.

Matte photograph paper has a dull or non-shiny finish that is the right side for printing.

The Printer's Paper Option

If your printer gives you a paper option, take the time to select the paper you are using. It really does make a difference in your finished print. Most problems with blurry or striped printouts can be attributed to selecting the wrong type of paper. Printer manufacturers package their own paper with their brand name on it. The paper is produced specially to work with their printer functions. This paper is more expensive than all-purpose brands. If possible, and if it is within your budget, you'll get optimum results if you use branded paper.

Does Size Matter?

You have two options when selecting the background paper for your scrapbook page—8½ x 11-inch (21.3 x 27.5 cm) and 12 x 12-inch (30 x 30 cm). Paper size doesn't matter when you're printing out photos, die cuts, clip art, or frames, since you will print them out on 8½ x 11-inch paper, then cut them out to the size you need. And, you can adjust the proportions you need before you print. However, when it comes to creating totally digital pages that you want to print out, there can be a few problems.

Currently there is no consumer scanner that can scan 12 x 12-inch pages as a whole. Professionally, there are such scanners, but few of us have access or want to spend a lot of money getting this size. If you can wait, it's just a matter of time until manufacturers produce these scanners for the scrapbook market at a reasonable price.

Epson does have software that will let you scan a 12 x 12 page in two parts and then blend or bleed the two images back together. Epson and Hewlett Packard both have a printer that will print the 12 x 12 papers. Just be aware that supplies and accessories are limited and often hard to locate to purchase.

You can design digital 12 x 12 scrapbook pages by adjusting the Page Set Up in your word processing program by changing the Paper Size to 12 x 12. You can make the same adjustments if you are creating in a photo editing software.

Here is a comparison between 8½ x 11-inch and 12 x 12-inch papers:

8½ x 11 (21.3 x 27.5 cm)
- Large variety of colors, patterns, designs
- Large variety in types of paper like vellum, handmade, or mulberry
- Large variety of albums and page protectors
- Easily adapted to digital
- Can run through any printer
- Can be easily scanned by any scanner
- Can be mounted onto a 12 x 12 paper

12 x 12 (30 x 30 cm)
- Large variety of colors, patterns, designs
- Larger area for design and photos
- Can be cut down to the smaller 8½ x 11 size
- More of a scrapbook feel
- Can be adapted to digital with the right equipment
- Needs printer able to print a 12 x 12-inch paper
- Can't be easily scanned as a whole, must be done in two scans and reassembled digitally

Some specialty papers will add new dimensions to your scrapbook pages by helping you create effects not available with standard papers. They are:

Fabric paper has a paper backing that allows you to feed it through most printers. Once printed, you remove the paper backing. You can create great digital elements or even a whole page with this paper, and, if you are ambitious, even a quilt or pillow.

Canvas is a heavyweight, highly textured paper that gives a rich oil-painting effect to a printed image.

Magnet paper is a very thin sheet magnet with a white paper topside. You can easily cut it with scissors after you print on the topside.

Cling paper, as its name suggests, will cling to most smooth surfaces. It is made from a thin plastic and has a right side for printing.

Decal paper lets you create and print your own decals that you can permanently adhere to a smooth surface.

Shrink plastic is a clear or opaque sheet of plastic that you can print on and then shrink, by baking it in the oven, to approximately 70 percent of its original size. You cannot use shrink plastic in many laser printers.

Acetate or transparency sheets are thin, lightweight, clear plastic sheets that you print on directly. They are often used for overhead projector presentations. This type of paper does have a right side for printing. Transparency paper comes in two types-one for laser printers and one for ink-jets.

Transfer paper, usually a heavyweight paper with a paper backing, allows you to transfer your printed image onto a T-shirt or tote bag using an iron. You can get some great effects for scrapbook pages using this paper. After allowing the transfer to cool, known as cold process, you remove the paper backing. Note: avoid using hot-process transfer paper, since you need to remove the paper backing from the transfer while it is hot.

Label paper comes in a huge variety. You can find label sheets for everything from a return address to labels for diskettes and CDs. You can even find label sheets that you can cut up. These are great for making your own self-stick digital die cuts. Finishes for this paper include photo quality, glossy, matte, and colored.

Top or Bottom Feed?

You need to know how your printer feeds the paper through its system as it prints. This is necessary especially when a paper has a right side, meaning you want to print on a specific side of the paper. Printers are either top or bottom feeding. Top feeds require you to place paper towards the back top of the printer. When using a top feed printer, you will want the right side (the printable side) facing you as you load it into the printer.

Bottom feeding printers usually have a paper tray at the front bottom of the printer. You can fill the tray with paper, but keep in mind that heavyweight and some specialty papers should be fed into a bottom-feeding printer one at a time. When using a bottom-feeding printer, the right side is facedown in the tray. Read the owner's manual to double-check what types of papers can be used in your printer. Manufacturers will state if a specific type of paper cannot be used in their printer.

THINK INK

Since the ink cartridge is one of the most expensive supply items you will need for digital scrapbooking, many printers allow you to select the amount of ink to use. The amount of ink determines the quality of print based on a scale that moves from lighter to darker, known as *draft, normal,* or *best.* In most cases before you do a final print, you should run a print test in black ink and in draft quality. That way you can check your sizing or placement without wasting costly ink.

If you are making copies of scrapbook pages or creating a mini scrapbook as a keepsake for family and friends (see the project on page 106), then you should select the normal to best ink quality. Test both settings and see which gives you the best results. In some printers you can't really see a difference between normal and best quality, but the normal setting will save some ink.

When you are printing photos you want to use as part of a traditional scrapbook page, you will want the best quality of ink. Many papers now include information on its packaging that recommends the type of paper or ink quality that gives the best results for different uses.

SPECIALTY PRINTING

With photo-printing software you can print the photo you want in the size that you want. With a few clicks of your mouse you can print a contact sheet, two 5 x 7-inch (12.5 x 17.5 cm), or a handful of wallet-size photos.

Printing a Contact Sheet

In your files, find the photos you want to use and click Print.

Either open your photo-printing software or click on a photo within a folder that will be one of the photos printed.

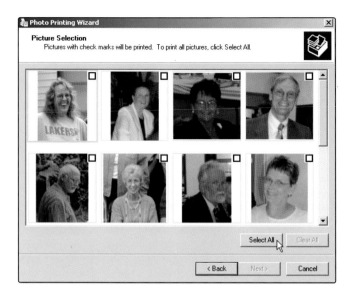

3 The program will ask you which photos within the folder you wish to print. Select all you wish to have on the contact sheet.

5 Click Next, and then select Contact Sheet, then print it. Store your contact sheets in a folder or binder.

4 Click next, and you'll select your printer if you have more than one on your system. This is a good time to double-check your printer properties or preferences. Make sure the correct paper is selected. Select whether you want draft, regular, or top-quality print.

Designing Signature Labels

Every scrapbook page should have a signature label on its back. It's fun to add this extra spark of creativity to your pages and albums. Just like a quilt's signature patch, a scrapbook's signature label should include the creator's name and date when the page was made. You can also coordinate these labels with a particular scrapbook you might be making like a heritage album, wedding album, or baby album. Labeling software allows you to easily create your labels.

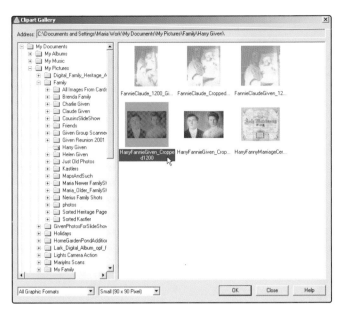

3 First select the file in which you want to insert or import an image or graphic. This will open a browser so you can find the file or folder that holds your image. Find the image you want, and click to insert.

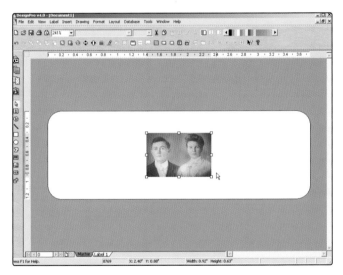

4 Move the image to where you want to place it within the label's design.

1 Open labeling software, and select the correct type of label you want to design.

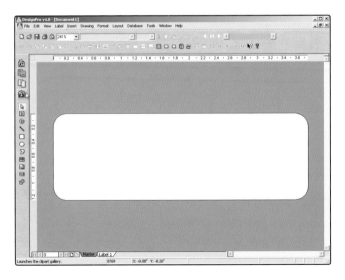

2 This example started with a blank label that is a glossy, photo-quality, ink-jet address label.

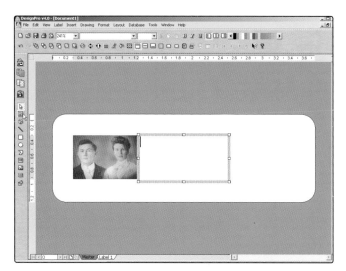

5 Now click your mouse to add text. A text box will appear. You can move this box around for better placement.

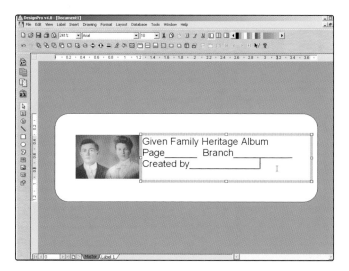

6 Type in your text. Remember, you can change to any available font, change size as you need, and even have colored text if printing on a color printer.

7 Print it! This is a good time to make sure you have all the right printer preferences.

The program will also ask you how many labels or sheets of labels you wish to print. You'll also have an option of what position should be the start position of the label. This option comes in handy if you want to print several different designs. You'd have Design 1 start at the first position, Design 2 start at the fourth position, and so on.

Reflections

Why is it when a baby is born, one of the first things we say is, "She has her father's chin," or, "He has his grandmother's eyes?" It's mostly a matter of family pride and joy. But more so, it's the wonderful awareness of seeing the past becoming the future, and that those who went before continue to live in us. This project reflects your family in you.

MATERIALS

Greeting card blank with 9 square windows

Fresco or chalk-pigment ink in color of your choice

Photos for contact sheet

Photo paper

Shiny metallic cardstock in color of your choice

Solid-color cardstock in color of your choice

Photo for inside of card

2 acid-free decorative papers in colors of choice

5 heart brads

SOFTWARE AND TOOLS

Scissors or craft knife

Sponge

Printer

Acid-free tape

Adhesive

Paper punch, awl, or eyelet-hole tool

Word-processing/journaling software

INSTRUCTIONS

1. Purchase a greeting card blank with nine square windows. If you can't find one, you can substitute by cutting the windows out of an uncut card blank, or you can make your own card blank from cardstock, then cut out the windows.

Designer: Maria Nerius

2. Using the sponge, apply the fresco or chalk pigment ink to the front of the card by lightly bouncing the inked sponge to cover the front of the card. I used green ink to coordinate with my selection of decorative papers. Set the card aside to dry.

3. Print a contact sheet of photos. Most printing software includes an option to print out photos as a contact sheet-usually around 36 images per photo sheet (see page 99). Trim the photos so you have at least nine to fill each card window. For this project, I selected older photos of my cousins.

4. Position the card to allow you to look at its front while you work. Working with one photo at a time, fit each photo into its own window. Tape each photo down.

5. To cover the tape and back of the photos, cut a square of the shiny metallic cardstock to a size that is big enough to cover the inside front, then adhere in place.

6. For the larger photo inside the card, you may already have a photo that is the size you need. If not, scan the photo you want, and bring it into your photo-editing software to resize and crop, if necessary. Adhere this photo to the inside of the card.

7. Select one of your decorative papers as the background paper. Create a layered mat with the solid-color cardstock on the bottom, the metallic cardstock in the middle, and the other decorative paper on top. Using a paper punch, awl, or or eyelet-hole tool, punch a hole in each corner of the solid-color mat, and insert a heart-shaped brad.

8. To create the upside-down, mirrored journaling, type the text in PowerPoint using a text box. Then type it in again in a new text box below the first. Use the Rotating option in Draw to "flip" the text in the new text box. If you do not have PowerPoint, you can use

our word-processing software to create your journaling, then use a copier to create a similar effect. When finished, trim the journaling as needed, and mat it on the metallic cardstock.

9. Center and adhere the card to the three-layered mat. Position the mat with the card on the upper portion of the background paper.

10. Determine your placement for the matted journaling on the background paper. Using an awl, paper punch, or eyelet-hole tool, punch a hole through the center of the journaling and through the background paper. Insert a heart brad through the hole. Note that the brad is adhering the journaling. The journaling can be twirled!

Contact Sheet Cards

You'll find that there are many different ways to use your photos printed as contact sheets. This variation of Reflections on page 102, lets you create cards that become miniature scrapbook greetings.

MATERIALS

Greeting card blank with 9
  square windows
Chalk ink in color of choice
Photos for contact sheet
Photo paper
Cardstock in color of your
  choice
Embellishments (optional)

SOFTWARE & TOOLS

Scissors or craft knife
Sponge
Printer
Acid-free tape
Acid-free adhesive
Acid-free markers (optional)

Designer: Maria Nerius

INSTRUCTIONS

1. Purchase a greeting card blank with nine square windows. If you can't find one, you can substitute by cutting the windows out of an uncut card blank, or you can make your own card blank from cardstock, then cut out the windows.

2. Using the sponge, apply the fresco or chalk pigment ink to the front of the card by lightly bouncing the inked sponge to cover the front of the card. Set the card aside to dry.

3. Print a contact sheet of photos. Select nine photos to fill the card's windows, then trim the photos from the contact sheet.

4. Working with one photo at a time, fit each photo into its own window to create a frame around the photo. Tape each photo from the back.

5. Cover the tape and back of the photos. Cut a square of cardstock to a size big enough to cover the inside front of the card, then adhere in place.

6. If you desire, use acid-free markers to add interest to the cards by drawing lines or designs. You can also embellish the front of the card with small charms, buttons, grommets, or stickers.

Signature Labels

Leave your mark, and do it beautifully. Signing your pages not only tells of the pride you take in your work, but will also provide future generations with valuable information about your handiwork.

MATERIALS

Photos or graphics
Labels

SOFTWARE & TOOLS

Label software
Printer

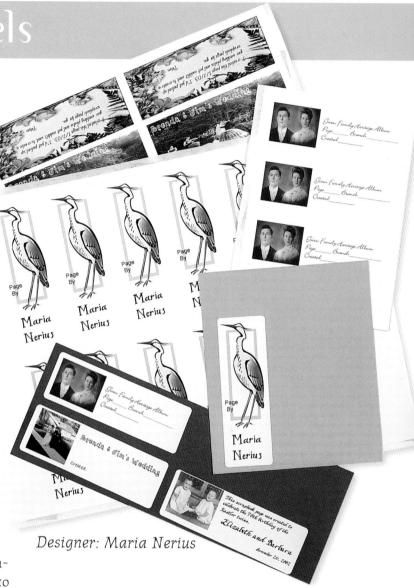

Designer: Maria Nerius

INSTRUCTIONS

1. Open your label software, and select the size and type of label you will be using. You may be given a choice to create a label from scratch or by a template feature within the software. If working by template, just import your graphic or photo into that box, and type the text into the text box provided. If creating from scratch, proceed with the instructions. Note: I created all the samples shown from scratch.

2. Using the software toolbar, open a graphics box. Using the cursor, adjust the placement and size of the box. Import your photo or graphic.

3. Using the software toolbar, open a text box. Using the cursor, adjust the placement and size of the box. Type in your text, and save the label.

4. Place a sheet of labels into your printer, making sure the right side of the sheet is in the correct position for your style of printer. Remember that top- and bottom-feeding printers load differently.

5. Print the labels. You will have a choice of how many labels will be printed per sheet of labels. You may wish to print a whole sheet of one design or print half a sheet of Design A and the other half Design B. Make your selections, and click Print.

Generation of Cousins

You'll find that these will be a big hit at any family reunion. Printing your photos wallet-sized makes them a perfect fit for a mini journal. After creating the title in your word processing program, have fun adding embellishments to make unique gifts for handing out to your own generation of cousins.

MATERIALS

Mini journals
Assortment of papers for matting
Photo and bright-white computer paper
Embellishments—brass charms and raffia

SOFTWARE & TOOLS

Word processing program
Photo-printing software/photo-editing
   software
Printer
Paper glue
Scissors

Designer: Maria Nerius

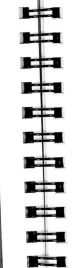

INSTRUCTIONS

1. The covers of these mini journals were all created with basic word processing software. Use the software to create titles for the front of the journal. Select different fonts. For added dimension, experiment with using the text with the rectangle and oval Draw features.

2. Save and print. Trim titles, and mat on coordinating paper.

3. Print your photos using the Wallet selection for photo printing. This will give you nine photos per sheet of photo paper. Trim photos, and mat with coordinating paper.

4. Glue the title to the front of the journal. Adhere the photos to the inside of journal.

5. Finish by adhering brass charms, tie a bow with raffia, or embellish as you wish.

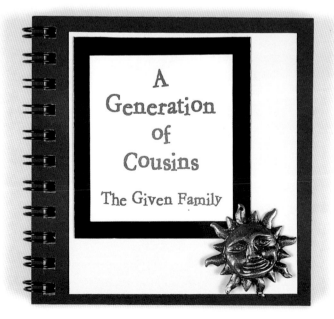

A
Generation
of
Cousins

The Given Family

USING THE INTERNET

Are you surfing the waves of the Web? Access to the World Wide Web means you have a treasure chest of creative and educational opportunities available to you to incorporate into your scrapbooking. I've referred to the Web several times in the book already, but let's concentrate solely on the Web for now.

First, you need a service provider like AOL, RoadRunner, or Earth Link. Then you have to be able to access this service either through a dial up service, a cable modem or a DSL (Data Subscriber Line) offered by your phone company.

Once you have access to the Web, you'll want to find sites that cover your creative interests. The fastest way to find scrapbooking sites is by using a search engine. Let's take a step-by-step look at finding, downloading, unzipping, and using a font provided free to all on a website.

FINDING FREE FONTS

When you purchase fonts as a software package, all you need to do is install the program and open up your word processing software to find and use the fonts. However, if you are downloading a font from a Web site on the Internet, you often will encounter the need to unzip a zipped file, since most fonts you find on the Web are zipped or compressed, which allows you to quickly download the font folder. You'll usually find unzipping instructions (including where to go to download a zip program) on the website where you found the font, but here's a quick primer on unzipping a zipped file.

You'll need to have a software program that unzips the folder so you can use it. If you are

This font found on the Web complements the news-bulletin theme of this page.

using a current Windows operating system, the unzipping software is already embedded into your system. You will just need to find the unzip feature and click on it. Or you can download a zip/unzip program from the Web. Font files are not the only files or folders that are zipped. Sometimes large graphics are zipped too.

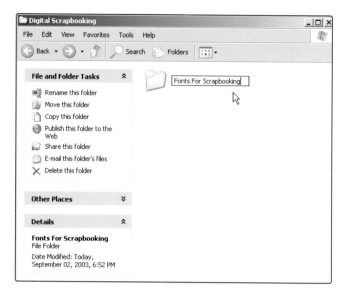

Create a folder to hold your download.

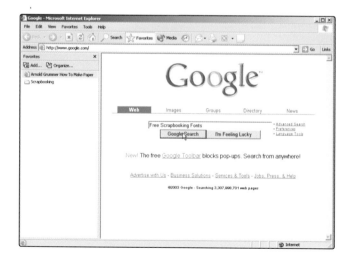

2 Use your favorite search engine to find web-sites that have downloadable fonts. Use key-words like: Scrapbooking Fonts or Free Fonts. The search engine will list sites that have fonts.

A Word about Viruses and Spyware

Viruses can be as simple as an e-mail message that, once opened, will send the same message to every e-mail address listed in your computer. Or they can be so horrific as to destroy your entire computer system.

There are several anti-virus software programs that can protect your computer. They are a wise investment if you rely on e-mail or download from the Internet. Software like McAfee or PC-cillin scans all e-mail, attachments, and downloads for viruses, and will either delete the virus or warn you about it so you can delete it.

Spyware is software attached to cookies or comes attached to a download. Every time you land on a website, it makes a cookie, which is information about you and your use of the computer. The spy-ware reports information back to the website.

Many feel this is an invasion of privacy, and the spyware can sometimes tie up your computer sys-tem. It's not always easy to find once installed. Just keep in mind that every time you download from the Web, you may be downloading more than you wanted.

Here are some websites that contain information about viruses, hoaxes, and spyware.

http://www.vmyths.com/
http://www.howstuffworks.com/virus.htm
http://www.hicom.net/~oedipus/virus32.html
http://www.spychecker.com/

4 You'll be asked if you wish to open the file or save the file. Select Save.

5 Your computer will then ask you where you wish to locate the downloaded font. This example shows that a Font Folder was created under My Documents. Double click the Font Folder to open it, and the selected font file will be downloaded into the folder.

3 You'll have to check out the different sites listed until you find some fonts you wish to download (top). Most sites will give you instructions for downloading and installing the fonts. In most cases you'll just double click your mouse on your selection to start the downloading process (bottom).

6 Close your Web connection, and find the font file. This example placed the LD Party font folder in a folder named Fonts.

7 The screen box will now show the file for the LD Party font. Click on Next to start the installation.

CLIP ART GALORE

You can also find free clip art on the Web. You'll use the same steps as finding and downloading fonts, but in most cases, clip art images are not zipped. You might want to check your word processing software and your photo-editing software for features that include some already-installed clip art images and the ability to get additional clip art from the manufacturer's website.

Over 10,000 free clip art images in over 300 categories...

Anatomy (93)
Animals (376)
Astrology (25)
Buildings - Houses (61)
Cartoons (5)
Computers (42)
Construction (41)
Credit Cards (13)
Dancing Ballet (46)
Email (58)
Entertainment (14)
Fantasy (15)
Flags (261)
Food (137)
Games (5)
Holiday (96)
Household (35)
Icons (3,129)
Law (21)
Literature (70)
Medicine (65)

Military (29)
Misc (14)
Money (36)
Music (260)
Nature (48)
Office - Business (83)
Party (39)
People (21)
Religion (40)
Science (48)
Security - Locks (10)
Signs (31)
Space (39)
Special Collections (1,101)
Sports (105)
Technology (42)
Time (9)
Transportation (668)
Web Stuff (1,984)
Words - Tags (56)

I Do a search for free clip art, find an interesting site, and go there. This site has lots of categories to browse. Let's click on dancing.

2 Look through the images, select one, and double click.

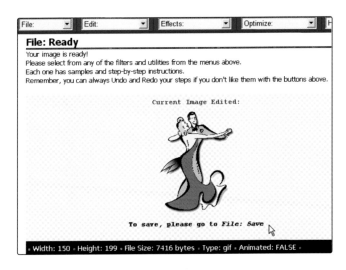

3 This site allows you some editing features; for example, you might prefer the image in black and white. To download the image, follow the site's instructions. In this cse, you'll o to file and click Save. You'll be given the option of where to place the clip art timage. make a folder to hold clip at or use your own organizational method.

FAMILY GENEALOGY RESOURCES

The Web is full of wonderful genealogy resources. From finding census reports to tracking down a map of France during the 1800s, there is interesting free information available to those of us with a few hours to kill surfing the Web.

Website addresses have a tendency to change or even disappear, so remember how to use a Web browser like you did to find free fonts.

Keywords like genealogy, a country's name like France or Italy, surname directory, military history, surname BBS (bulletin board service), family trees, and historic timelines will give you a long list of appropriate websites to search.

There are many genealogy websites that offer free family home pages. They give you the ability to upload a family tree for other family and friends to view. Many genealogy enthusiasts love to share information and will track public posts on public genealogy home pages and family trees trying to locate members in various family branches. A public home page or family tree will be included in the site's directory and often in the larger Web search engines. You have the option to make your home page public or private. Most websites will allow you to select a password to access the information, and you can share that password with family and friends.

The home pages and family trees are uploaded by following the templates and instructions given at each individual website. You may be given a few options for color and placement, but the uploading and designing is made easy by using the website's template.

You can also purchase family history and family tree software. You install the software into your computer and then begin to fill out the family information. The software can automatically sort and filter the data to create a family tree, a family pedigree, a descendant's chart, and an ancestor's chart. These are wonderful additions to any family heritage scrapbook. Not all family genealogy software is compatible, so if you plan on sharing information with other family members, you might want to make sure everyone is using the same or compatible software.

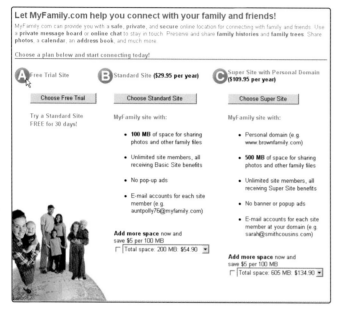

Do a Web engine search for websites that offer free Web pages. Once you've selected a site, you'll need to follow that site's instructions.

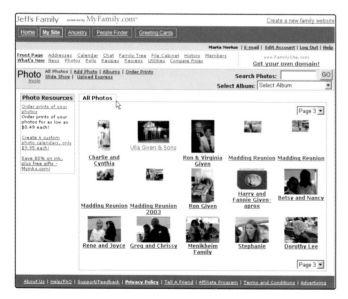

2 Select your preference for a page, and follow the instructions given on the site to create your own unique pages. This is my cousin Jeff's Given family website.

The Mother of All Genealogy Sites

www.cyndislist.com

Cyndi's List of Genealogy Sites on the Internet was started in March of 1996 by a genealogy enthusiast, and has grown to be one of the largest free genealogy sites on the Web. It is what is called a links site. The site lists hundreds of web sites according to categories, including beginner information, locations, immigration, migration, and so on. All you have to do is select a site of interest and click on it. You will be hyperlinked or redirected to the site you are interested in. You can also use the site's search engine to quickly locate any specific topic or subject.

Why is this site so special? Cyndi has basically taken all the legwork out of trying to filter through thousands of sites to find the topics that might interest you—this can save you hours and hours of time. Almost every imaginable subject is covered. You can find timelines from countries from Argentina to Wales. You can locate cemeteries and county seats, discover the roots of your family's religion and ethnic traditions, find out the history of your family's surname, or even locate a professional genealogist to do your family history for you.

This site is very interactive, which is as helpful to those just beginning to trace their roots as it is to amateur genealogists who have already traced their family branches back dozens of generations. This site also includes an expanse of computer information, such as educa-

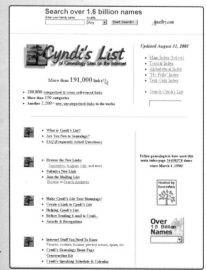

tional materials on viruses, mail lists, copyrights, and other computer issues.

CREATING A MAIL LIST AND HOME PAGE

Our scrapbook creations are just too wonderful to keep all to ourselves—we want to share our pages with others including family and friends. Today, that's not always easy, since families can be spread all over the world. Creating a mail list or home page is a simple way to easily share your scrapbook artistry with others. By scanning pages and uploading them to a mail list or home page, your pages can be seen by a quick click of the mouse. The community of scrapbookers who are a part of a mail list or create home pages is growing. This community is truly inspiring. You can learn from others who share your passion for scrapbooking, and they can be encouraged by you!

Enjoying a Mail List

Mail lists are a combination of a home page and an e-mail list. There are many websites for members, called e-groups or clubs that host free mail lists. To become a member of this type of website, all you need to do is fill out a brief information form that includes name, state, and e-mail address.

A mail list usually has a home or starting page and has an area where you can upload photos or graphics, plus it provides the ability for all members of the list to e-mail each other. You also have the option to read posted e-mails on the mail list from the web, so instead of receiving too much e-mail in your electronic mailbox, you can read the e-mails on the mail list site.

You can find a free mail list service by using your choice of Web search engines. You can create a private family mail list, which is a great way for your family members to keep in touch. Or you might want to create a public mail list to share your art, craft, and hobby talents. The possibilities are endless, and the upkeep of a mail list is minimal.

BASICS STEPS TO CREATING A MAIL LIST

Use a search engine to find a free mail list service. Check out a few of the different services for available features. Select a service, and start the process to create the mail list. You can see on this screen box that I'm a member of Yahoo Groups. The screen also displays the groups I'm a member of. Click Start a New Group.

Ideas for Mail Lists

Mail lists are an easy way to stay in touch with family and friends around the world. Can't think of a subject matter for your mail list? Here are a few suggestions:

- Class Reunions
- Photography
- Family Newsletter
- Craft or Hobby-scrapbooking or photography
- Personal or Professional Résumé
- Surname-genealogy
- Vacations

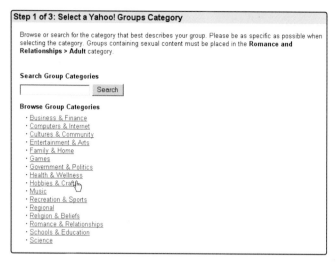

Step 1 of 3: Select a Yahoo! Groups Category

Browse or search for the category that best describes your group. Please be as specific as possible when selecting the category. Groups containing sexual content must be placed in the **Romance and Relationships > Adult** category.

Search Group Categories

[Search]

Browse Group Categories
- Business & Finance
- Computers & Internet
- Cultures & Community
- Entertainment & Arts
- Family & Home
- Games
- Government & Politics
- Health & Wellness
- Hobbies & Crafts
- Music
- Recreation & Sports
- Regional
- Religion & Beliefs
- Romance & Relationships
- Schools & Education
- Science

2 Select the category where you will place the mail list—categorizing a mail list makes it easier to find. Since this mail list will be about scrapbooking, Hobbies & Crafts is a good choice. However, selecting Family & Home is easily another good choice.

Browse Group Categories

Top > Hobbies & Crafts > **Crafts**   [Place my group in *Crafts*]

Select a more specialized subcategory
- Basketry
- Beading
- Blacksmithing
- Candlemaking
- Crocheting
- Egg Art
- Gourd Art
- Jewelry Making
- Knitting
- Lacemaking
- Leatherworking
- Macrame
- Needlecrafts
- Polymer Clay
- Quilting
- Rock Painting
- Rubber Stamping
- Rug Hooking
- Scrapbooks
- Sewing
- Soapmaking
- Spinning and Weaving
- Woodworking
- Ceramics
- Furniture Design
- Handcrafted Dolls
- Mail Art
- Origami

3 This mail list service continues to want the mail list categorized further. There is a category under Hobbies and Crafts for Scrapbooking, so that is selected.

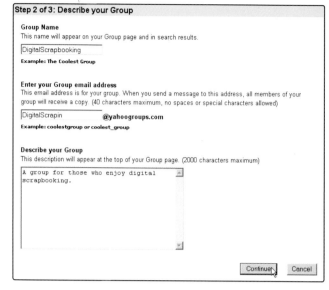

Step 2 of 3: Describe your Group

Group Name
This name will appear on your Group page and in search results.

[DigitalScrapbooking]

Example: The Coolest Group

Enter your Group email address
This email address is for your group. When you send a message to this address, all members of your group will receive a copy. (40 characters maximum, no spaces or special characters allowed)

[DigitalScrapin]   @yahoogroups.com

Example: coolestgroup or coolest_group

Describe your Group
This description will appear at the top of your Group page. (2000 characters maximum)

A group for those who enjoy digital scrapbooking.

[Continue] [Cancel]

4 Now the fun begins. Select a name for the mail list, create an e-mail address, and write a brief description of what the mail list will be about. Fill in the information, and click Continue.

Congratulations!

Your Group **DigitalScrapin** has been created. You can access your group using the link below or from the Yahoo Groups "My Groups" page.

Group name: DigitalScrapin
Group home page: http://groups.yahoo.com/group/DigitalScrapin
Group email: DigitalScrapin@yahoogroups.com

Customize Your Group
Choose who can join, who can post messages, and more!

[Customize Group]

Invite People to Join
Grow your group now! Invite friends, family, and colleagues.

[Invite People]

5 The mail list is created. Remember to write down all the information about your mail list, including the website address and e-mail address.

Customize DigitalScrapin

This wizard will help you customize your Yahoo Group. You can decide

- whether or not to list your group in Yahoo! Groups directory
- who is able to join your group
- who can post messages to the group and how
- whether or not messages are archived
- what web features your group will use

There are three simple steps. For more information about a step, click on "Learn More" where available. You can modify these settings later in the "Management" section of your Group page.

[Get Started] [Cancel]

6 You can now customize your mail list.

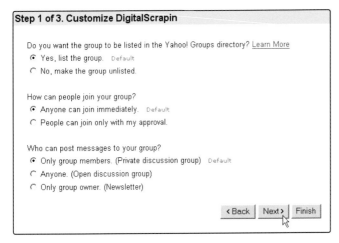

Step 1 of 3. Customize DigitalScrapin

Do you want the group to be listed in the Yahoo! Groups directory? Learn More
○ Yes, list the group.   Default
○ No, make the group unlisted.

How can people join your group?
○ Anyone can join immediately.   Default
○ People can join only with my approval.

Who can post messages to your group?
○ Only group members. (Private discussion group)   Default
○ Anyone. (Open discussion group)
○ Only group owner. (Newsletter)

[< Back] [Next >] [Finish]

DigitalScrapin · DigitalScrapbooking   Group Owner [Edit My Membership]

© CreditCards.com
CLICK HERE
for the best Credit Card
offers!

▶ **Home**
Messages
  Pending
  Post
Chat
Files
Photos
Links
Database
Polls
Members
  Pending
Calendar

Promote
Invite

Management

★ = Owner
☆ = Moderator
@ = Online

Description   Category: Scrapbooks
A group for those who enjoy digital scrapbooking.

Most Recent Messages

No messages for this group.

Group Email Addresses

Post message: DigitalScrapin@yahoogroups.com
Subscribe: DigitalScrapin-subscribe@yahoogroups.com
Unsubscribe: DigitalScrapin-unsubscribe@yahoogroups.com
List owner: DigitalScrapin-owner@yahoogroups.com

Membership
You are a moderator of this group

[Edit My Membership]
[Leave Group]

Pending Activity
0 Members
0 Messages

Group Info
Members: 1
Founded: Sep 3, 2003
Language: English

Group Settings
· Listed in directory
· Open membership
· All messages require approval
· All members may post
· Archives for members only
· Email attachments are permitted

7 You can decide if you want this to be a public mail list that anyone can join or a private mail list where you will invite whom you want to join. You can let e-mail messages be posted automatically or select to approve any e-mail before it is posted.

9 By using the website's templates, you can create a home page for the mail list. You can insert photos and even select the color theme. Above is the basic home page before it was customized.

Step 3 of 3. Customize DigitalScrapin

Who should the message archives be available to? Learn More
○ All members can view archives.   Default
○ Only moderators can view archives.
○ Anyone can view archives.
○ Messages are not archived.

Who should be able to access the following web features?

Chat	Members ▾
Files and photos	Members ▾
Links	Members ▾
Database	Members ▾
Polls	Members ▾
Member listing	Members ▾
Calendar	Members ▾
Promote	Members ▾

8 Mail lists can include databases, links, chats, polls, and calendars. You decide who can contribute to these features.

DigitalScrapin · DigitalScrapbooking   Group Owner [Edit My Membership]

© CreditCards.com
CLICK HERE
for the best Credit Card
offers!

Home
Messages
  Pending
  Post
Chat
Files
Photos
Links
Database
Polls
Members
  Pending
Calendar

Promote
Invite

▶ Management

★ = Owner
☆ = Moderator
@ = Online

Group Settings   Management Help

Back to Management

Web Address [Edit]

Web Address : http://groups.yahoo.com/group/DigitalScrapin

Description [Edit]

Title : DigitalScrapbooking
Description : A group for those who enjoy digital scrapbooking.
Related Link : None selected
Primary Language : English
Listing Type : Listed in Yahoo! Groups directory

Category [Edit]

This category determines where listed groups appear in the directory. Unlisted groups are not visible in the directory.
Category : Hobbies & Crafts > Crafts > **Scrapbooks**

Colors and Photo

Colors [Edit]   Photo [Edit]

Left Header Sub-header Accent Row Color Background   No Photo

10 Click the editing button.

Save Changes | Reset | Cancel

Colors

○ **Yahoo!**

Left	Header	Sub-header	Accent	Row Color	Background

○ **Classic**

Left	Header	Sub-header	Accent	Row Color	Background

○ **Summertime**

Left	Header	Sub-header	Accent	Row Color	Background

◉ **Tee Off**

Left	Header	Sub-header	Accent	Row Color	Background

○ **Splash**

Left	Header	Sub-header	Accent	Row Color	Background

○ **Plum**

Left	Header	Sub-header	Accent	Row Color	Background

○ **Sahara**

Left	Header	Sub-header	Accent	Row Color	Background

○ **Custom** [Edit]

Left	Header	Sub-header	Accent	Row Color	Background

Save Changes | Reset | Cancel

11 You can select a new color theme.

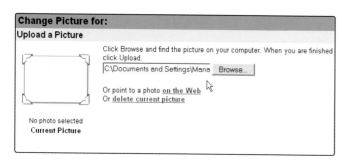

Change Picture for:

Upload a Picture

Click Browse and find the picture on your computer. When you are finished click Upload.

C:\Documents and Settings\Marie [Browse...]

Or point to a photo **on the Web**
Or **delete current picture**

No photo selected
Current Picture

12 You can insert a photo from your files.

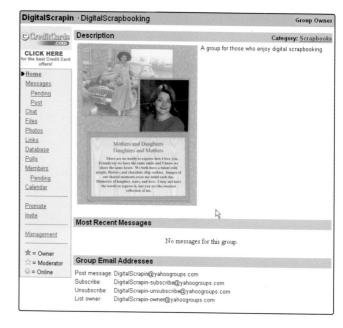

13 Click to save the changes, and you have your customized mail list. Come join my mail list, Digital Scrapin, at:

http://groups.yahoo.com/group/DigitalScrapin/

CREATING A HOME PAGE

Most Internet access providers like AOL, Earth-Link, or RoadRunner provide a certain amount of space within their websites for members to create a free home page. It can be as simple or complex as you want it to be, but either way, it's fun to have your own spot on the World Wide Web. Creating the home page is similar to creating a mail list. A home page isn't quite as interactive as a mail list, although some home pages can include a chat room or a bulletin board for posting messages.

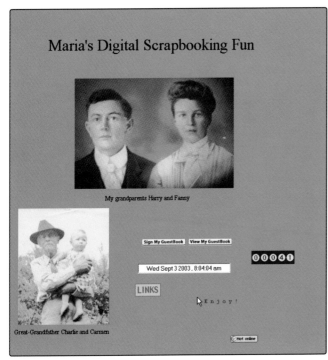

Find a free home page service-you can do a search. Then follow the templates and instructions for creating your own home page at the site.

Remember to write down the web address of your home page and your password for the page. Most free services require you to maintain the site, which means you need to update, edit, and have some traffic (people viewing the site) a few times a year. Visit my homepage and sign my guest book at www.geocities.com/minerius/first.html

E-MAIL

We all know that e-mail is a great way to stay in touch with family and friends, but when you share your photos and scrapbook pages, your messages come to life. Keep in mind what you know about JPEGs, since you will need to send as small a photo or graphic file as possible. Some e-mail services just can't handle large files, and some files can be too big for electronic transfer. Make sure that you scan and photograph in JPEG format. The photo or graphic will still look great when viewed on the screen, and in most cases will print with some quality.

Open your e-mail program. Select New Mail, and fill in the e-mail address. You can write any text in the e-mail as you normally would. When finished, you'll attach the file you wish to send, which can be a photo, graphic, or even a scanned or digital scrapbook page. Find the Attachment button or feature on your e-mail tool bar, and click it.

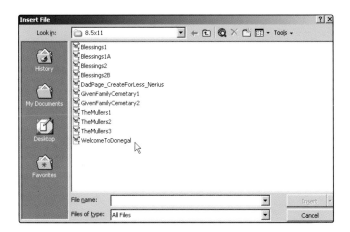

2 Clicking the Attachment button or feature allows you to browse your folders to find the file (photo or graphic) you want to attach to your e-mail. By attaching the file, you will send a copy of that file along with your e-mail. Find the file, and click Insert. The file is now attached to the e-mail. Click Send.

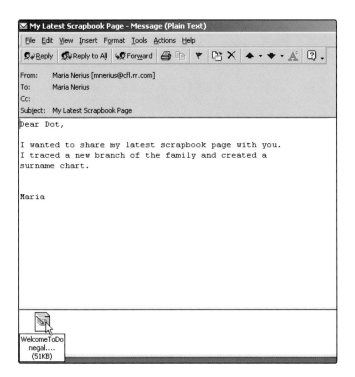

3 On the other end, all that needs to be done is for the recipient to open the e-mail, and click on the attached file to open it.

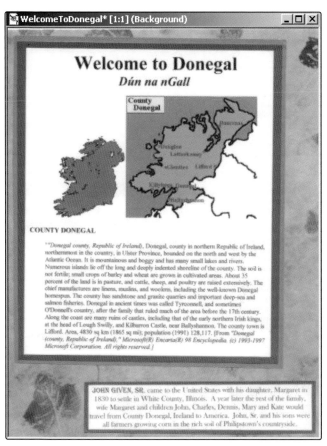

4 Your selected or default graphics software will open and let you view the photo.

Cory's Smile

We always say Cory is as busy as a bee, and that his smile is like sunshine—which made creating the theme for his page a snap. All I had to do was find the right clip-art image for framing his photo. You'll find that this page is fast and easy!

MATERIALS

Clip art or image art software
Photo
Red cardstock or vellum
Background paper
Stick-on letters
Embellishments

SOFTWARE & TOOLS

Printer
Scanner
Photo-editing software
Word-processing/Journaling
    software (optional)

INSTRUCTIONS

1. This sample used an image purchased as one of a collection on CD. You may find a frame template you prefer on CDs or on the Web. Select an image and print it. I used photo paper for a high-gloss look.

2. This photo was scanned and enlarged from a regular-size print. I cropped in tight on the scanner so the photo really captured Cory's smile.

3. You can decide whether you want the image (frame) printout to also serve as the background paper. I chose to make this a 12 x 12-inch (30 x 30 cm) page by cutting out the frame and adhering it to a piece of 12 x 12-inch background paper.

Designer: Maria Nerius & Terry Taylor

4. Mat the photo onto cardstock or vellum. Trim as needed.

5. Adhere the matted photo to the center, toward the top, of the frame image.

6. You can create the title using your word-processing or journaling software. Here, I liked the look of the bright red stick-on letters.

7. Adhere embellishments of your choice.

Samantha & Ken

This simple but pretty page is created by printing clip art and matting the clip art to create a border. Adding the block embellishments and a few pastel buttons in between the clip art complements the color of the papers used for the background and matting.

MATERIALS

1 sheet yellow linen paper
Coordinating decorative and solid papers
Acid-free adhesive
Photo
Embellishments—small buttons and stick-on baby blocks

SOFTWARE & TOOLS

Clip art or image art software
Printer
Photo-editing software (optional)
Word processing/journaling software
Scissors or paper trimmer

INSTRUCTIONS

1. Print out your selection of clip art. This project used images from a purchased CD. Before printing, you may have to resize the images in your photo-editing software. Or, you can use printing software that allows you to print wallet-size images or contact sheets (see page 98). For this project, I printed out the images as a contact sheet. Trim the images as needed.

2. Mat each image with coordinating decorative or solid papers. Trim to leave just a slight border.

Designer: Maria Nerius

3. Use your word-processing or journaling software to create the title, then print. Note that this project includes a date just under the title in smaller print. Mat the title as desired—I chose to triple mat.

4. Since the photo was taken with a digital camera. I opened the photo in my photo-editing software to crop and enlarge it. Then I printed it on matte photo paper.

5. Mat the photo with coordinating decorative papers. The photo is double matted.

6. Cut a strip of solid coordinating paper to approximately 1 x 11½ inches (2.5 x 28.8 cm). Adhere this strip vertically onto background yellow linen paper approximately 1 inch (2.5 cm) in from the left side.

7. Adhere the matted clip art images onto the strip as shown. Adhere the photo, centering it toward the top and between the border and right edge. Adhere the title. Add your embellishments.

To Kiss an Elephant

MATERIALS

Clip art or image software
Photo paper
Photos
Sheet of ivory cardstock
Coordinating decorative papers
Rubber stamps—used here: letters and kiss stamp

SOFTWARE & TOOLS

Photo-editing software
Printer
Scissors or paper trimmer
Acid-free adhesive
Stamp pad

The perfect theme creates a framework for a special memory. This clip art frame worked double time by providing a cutout motif to balance the design.

Designer: Maria Nerius & Terry Taylor

INSTRUCTIONS

1. Find a clip-art frame that complements the subject of the scrapbook page. This project uses a square image with a jungle theme .

2. Print the frame in actual size (the size it is on the software) on matte photo paper.

3. Using photo-editing software, size the photo to fit the frame. Note that sizing the photo a bit larger than the frame opening allows you to adhere the photo to the wrong side of the frame. When you resize, make sure that the major action of the photo fits in the frame opening, then print.

4. Cut out the inside of the frame. Trim photo if necessary, and adhere to the back of the frame. Then adhere the frame to the top left of the off-white cardstock that serves as the background paper.

5. In word-processing or journaling software, create journaling and print on a coordinating paper, then trim and adhere to the matting.

6. Open the frame in your photo-editing software. Resize the frame—for this project I tripled the size—and print.

7. Select a motif from the frame, and cut it out. Use it as a matted decorative motif in the lower left-hand corner.

8. Create a title using word-processing or journaling software. Rubber-stamp letters and a kiss stamp complete the theme.

Internet Scrapbooking

Out of time? If you have the perfect picture but just can't find the time to make a page, send it along and share the fun. A scrapbooking grandma miles away will welcome the chance to not only see the picture but make a page. Then she can return the favor—by scanning the finished page, she can send you a digital copy that you can keep in a digital scrapbook or print out for your memory album.

Designer: Terry Taylor

MATERIALS

Photo
Decorative paper
Sheet of sandpaper
6 square grommets
2 small tags
Stick-on letters
Shells

SOFTWARE & TOOLS

Photo-editing software
Printer
Decorative edge scissors
Acid-free adhesive
Grommet tool

INSTRUCTIONS

1. If needed, bring the photo into your photo-editing software to resize. Print out the photo.

2. Using your decorative edge scissors, cut the decorative paper slightly larger than the photo.

3. Adhere the photo to the decorative paper. Position the matted photo on the sandpaper. Grommet on the four corners of the photo.

4. Cut pieces of decorative paper and adhere to the tags. Use the stick-on letters for the title and caption. Position the tags where desired, and grommet through their holes.

5. Place shells around the photos, and adhere.

Family Heritage Motif Papers

From one simple motif, you can make three coordinating papers. I found this worked best when making my family heritage pages. The motif provides a unity of theme—the tree representing my family tree—while the different designs give me the variety for creating many layouts.

Designer: Maria Nerius

MATERIALS

4 solid-color background papers
Sheet of green handmade paper
Sheet of coordinating paper

SOFTWARE & TOOLS

Paper punch—tree design
Acid-free adhesive
Scanner
Printer

Wedding Day of Claude & Helen
June 25, 1949
Harry Given, Wilma Given, Helen, Claude and John Given

Left Page Clockwise:
John Given 1891
Margaret Given 1902
Simon & Helene Obermaier 1928
Right Page Clockwise:
Helene 1926
Maggie Given 1896
James T. Given 1956

INSTRUCTIONS

1. Select a background paper. A solid neutral color works best-you want your photos to stand out, not the background paper.

2. For the first design-a tree at bottom left or bottom right-use the paper punch on either bottom side of the background paper. Set the punched-out tree aside. Cut out a small square of the green handmade paper and adhere it to the back of the background paper to cover the punch.

3. For the second design, use the tree from step 2. Cut a square of the handmade paper, and adhere the tree to the center. Adhere this matted tree to the center top of a background paper.

4. For the third design, punch trees out of coordinating paper. Adhere the trees in a random pattern or design onto a sheet of background paper.

5. You can scan your designs, then print out as many as you need to complete your scrapbook.

CHAPTER 4

Totally Digital Scrapbooking

You've already learned almost everything you need to know to create totally digital pages! This section of the book will help bring all those skills together so you can use your computer to make complete scrapbook pages on your screen—then the next step is to just click and print. This section will also help you learn how to create an entire scrapbook electronically. A dedicated scrapbooker will take advantage of both traditional and digital skills to round out her creativity.

Sharing the memories of this wedding was easy with an all digital page.

One of the best benefits of all digital pages is that you can work quickly and print out duplicates with ease. We all know that every page in a scrapbook doesn't have to be a masterpiece, but we do want to create a page that shows off the photos and is interesting to look at. As I wrote this book, I really began to appreciate how much time creating on my computer saves me, especially when I create family pages that I want to share with my ever-growing family. I was most impressed with creating a totally digital scrapbook that allowed me to bring in the element of sound with music and voice clips.

Digital scrapbooking was meant to complement our traditional forms of scrapbooking and memory albums. One thing to remember, as you consider adding a digital page or digital scrapbook to your collection, is that there's nothing more archival and acid free than electronic creativity and art. Your digital pages will have emotion and heart because you create each with care and love. It's just a different level of expression. Give totally digital a try! You'll get hooked!

CREATING DIGITAL PAGES USING WORD PROCESSING

The easiest way to begin designing an all-digital page is to use your word-processing software. This page will be saved as a text document file. Once saved, you can keep it in a file with other digital or scanned pages, print it and place it in an album, print multiples to send to family and friends, send the file as an attachment, or save it as an HTML file for use on a website.

1 Open your word-processing program. Type in a title, select the font, and center. If desired, select a color other than black. The specialty font used is CK Fishbones.

2 Import a graphic. This page will have two graphics. To import a photo, graphic, or clip art, you need to create the place where it will go on the page by drawing a text box.

3 The first graphic is a frame imported from the Microsoft website. I did a search in clip art, found my frame, checked the image, and downloaded it into my word processing program.

4 Insert the frame on the page and size it to the page if needed.

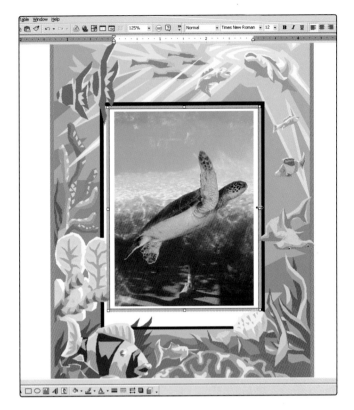

HTML, which is a program language used to create web pages. All you have to do is save the scrapbook page as a Web page instead of a document.

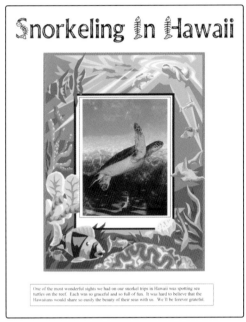

The finished page.

5 The second graphic is a photo I took while snorkeling in Hawaii. It was stored in my Vacations folder in My Pictures. I imported it and placed it into the clip art frame.

6 Add a text box for journaling, and type in the text.

When you're finished, you can save the page for future use, or print it. Your word processing software may also let you save the designed scrapbook page in a format that you can upload to the Web without the hassles of having to know

BURNING A CD

The best way to digitally save all your photographs, copies of your traditional scrapbook pages, and a digital scrapbook or slide show is to burn it onto a CD. Why a CD rather than a diskette? Remember memory? A CD holds roughly 600 times more than a diskette. A CD allows you to use high resolution and still be able to get dozens of images onto it.

If you do not already have it in your computer, you will need CD-burning software There is a variety of brands to choose from, so take your time and read all the features available to you. I like simple software rather than fancy features. I also like that I can use a step-by-step tutorial with my CD-burning software perfect for your own needs.

And a little friendly reminder about the CD drive you need for burning CDs—it must be a CD R/W, meaning the CD drive has the ability to write or burn CDs.

You'll want to pick out some CD labels and jewel box inserts. While you're shopping you might want to check out all the wonderful types of CDs you can burn. CDs come in standard size and also a mini- and business-card size. All three will fit into your CD R/W drive. CDs also come in an array of colors—so do jewel boxes!

Have some fun with it, and personalize your style right down to the CD itself. Note that it's the quality of the paper the label is made of that makes the difference, not the quality of your printer. I have learned that glossy paper CD labels do a much better job when you want to place a photo in the design. Matte finish CD labels work best for graphics, clip art, or simple color designs.

2 Click to burn the CD.

3 Click, hold, and drop files or folders to place them in the area of the screen box that holds the data to be burned.

1 Open the CD-burning software and select the file or folder you want burned onto the CD. This example used Nero Burning Rom software. Insert a blank CD into your CD Writer drive.

4 A new screen box will let you know the CD is being burned, and a new box will pop up when the process is complete.

MAKING CD AND JEWEL BOX LABELS

Now it's time to design the CD and jewel box labels. Here's a chance to truly personalize your creation, especially if you intend to give the CD as a gift to family or friends. I love doing this with photos I take at weddings, birthday parties for my godchildren, and family vacations. I feel it is a very special keepsake I can give to others.

Take as much care designing your CD label and jewel box as you would a scrapbook page.You will need separate software from the CD burner. The software I used was downloaded from the label manufacturer's site: www.avery.com.

The sample that follows is a CD and jewel box I made for a friend's 25th wedding anniversary. It included a digital scrapbook created by their children, a few movie clips from the surprise party (AVIs), and a digital slide show of the party photos. They loved it!

CD Stompers

You can peel the CD labels and stick them on by hand, but CD label stompers make applying the label worry free. Stompers make it less likely for you to wrinkle the label, and they also center the label with ease. The first style of CD stomper has a large center hole. The second has a smaller center hole (just slightly larger than the CD's hole). You'll need to get the coordinating style of label for each. You'll print your label and peel it from the paper backing. Lay the label front side down (adhesive side up) onto the stomper. Place your CD right side down (writeable side up), and press down. The label is now adhered smoothly onto the CD. You can find CD stompers wherever CD labels are sold.

CDs

For CDs there are two types of labels—one with a hole that goes right to the small hole of the CD, and the older version with a larger hole in it.

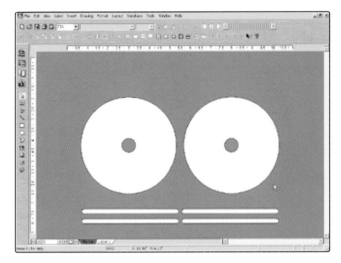

Open the label software. This example shows the more versatile CD label with the small hole. This software has handy templates to use if you don't want to create your own design, but using your own graphics and text makes the label so much more personal. On the toolbar you will find a button that will let you import a graphic. Click on the Import button.

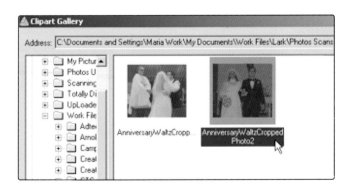

The import feature will allow you to browse your own graphics files. For this example, I used a photo of the couple's wedding day. Find your photo, and click OK.

3 The photo is now inserted or imported into your label software. Note that the size needs adjusting.

5 You can then add some text to your label. On the toolbar of the label software you will find a text option. Click it, and enter your text in the box.

4 To adjust the fit of the photo, first highlight it, then move the lines to make the photo bigger as you place it on the CD in the position you desire.

6 This software has a curved or circular text option that follows the shape of the CD. Once you select it, a guideline will appear on the image on the screen. This will make it easier for you to apply your text. Type in text, and click to apply. Then Print.

Jewel Box

Now we need to create a personalized cover and insert for the jewel box-an elegant name for those ordinary little plastic CD cases. You'll use the same labeling software you used for CDs to make the labels for the jewel box.

You'll be given the option to use a template or quick design. For the quick design, all you really need to do is print a premade insert or fill in the blank text boxes. But let's continue to make our own for a very personal design.

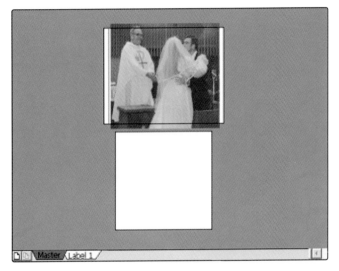

Find the photo you wish to use. Let the browser tool help you, then click OK on the selected image just like you did for the CD label.

You can add text by clicking on the text button. A small box will appear that you can enlarge to include the text you wish to add. This program gives you most of the text options found in any word processing program, including font, size, and color.

To finish the jewel case you need to complete the insert panel that is found below the cover panel. And add more text if you like. Then all you need to do is print and assemble the CD package.

ALL-DIGITAL SCRAPBOOKS

There are several ways to put together a digital scrapbook. First, you can store scrapbook pages in a word processing format so that the file will appear within a text document. Then you can place several files (individual pages) into a folder. To open the folder, you would click on each file to view the pages. There would be no transitions from one page to another, but technically, the folder is a digital scrapbook.

You could also create several digital pages or scan several traditionally constructed pages, then cut and paste each into one single file. You would then be able to scroll down the document, viewing the pages as a vertical scrapbook.

But the best way to create a digital scrapbook is to use software that is designed to recreate the total effect of a scrapbook with individual pages, including the visual effect of turning each page. Most of this software will let you incorporate digital images, borders, frames, clip art, and even sound.

You want to look for software features like photo editing, so you can edit a graphic within the program, or easy step-by-step CD burning. Please note that most scrapbooking software will not copy or burn a CD, but makes it an easy process to locate your own CD-writing software program. If you want to print a page or the entire scrapbook, make sure the digital scrapbook program allows you to print.

There are several digital scrapbook software programs available from E-Books, Adobe, and pcCrafters. The example you will see shortly was done with FlipAlbum 5 from E-books.

Most digital scrapbook programs include photo-editing features, but many lack advanced editing capabilities like red-eye correction or repair scratches.

For the best results, you will want to have a folder of photos that you have already corrected with your photo-editing software. In other words, make sure you crop and photo enhance each photo before placing it into the folder.

It's important to clearly name each photo so that you can recognize what the photo contains by reading the file name of the photo. When naming the photo file, take into consideration the order you want the photos to appear. Then place all the files into a single folder. This makes it easier to put together a digital scrapbook or slide show by inserting a folder that contains all the pictures. After you get the hang of putting together digital scrapbooks, you may prefer creating a blank album and inserting each element individually, but that takes more time than just inserting a folder.

CREATING A DIGITAL SCRAPBOOK

I've mentioned a few of the unique features of designing a digital scrapbook, but it bears repeating that digital scrapbooks offer you a way to incorporate everything you love about traditional scrapbooking—photos, color, design, decorative papers, and journaling—without having to get out the scissors, glue, and acid-free pens. You can add frames, borders, sound bits, and movie clips with a click of your mouse. You can increase a photo size, decrease a photo size, crop a photo, or rearrange your photos to your heart's content without taking up the entire dining room table. And the best benefit of all is that you can quickly burn a few copies onto CDs and mail out your latest creation without a huge expense.

One of the things I think about when deciding to create a traditional scrapbook (or scrapbook page) is, am I going to want to share it with others? Most of my own digital scrapbooks were created from photos taken at parties, birthdays, holidays, and family gatherings. Most of my family and friends have and use computers. And even those who don't own computers have someone close by who does. The example I've chosen to show you is from an annual family reunion on my dad's side of the family. I'd always wanted to create a family heritage scrapbook and knew it would be easy to gather up some family history and tradition at the reunion. It was the perfect way to combine the tradition of family past with the high tech of family future. Let's get digital!

Create a folder with the name of your scrapbook. Place all edited photos into this folder.

Open the digital scrapbook program. You will be given some options: Create a scrapbook from folder; Create a blank scrapbook; or Open existing scrapbook. Select Create From Folder, and click OK. A screen box will open that lets you browse through your folders. Find and select your

folder. This example used a folder named Family Reunion Scrapbook. Click OK.

3 Your new scrapbook will appear. The name of your scrapbook will be the name of your file.

4 You have the option to redesign the cover if you wish. You can change the title, the theme, and the color.

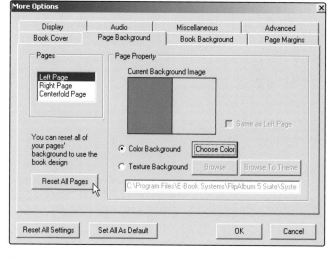

Digital Scrapbook Features

Now that it's time to complete the digital scrapbook design, let's check out some features. Instead of picking out papers at your local scrapbook store or craft shop, you'll be picking out digital backgrounds. The software I used for this digital scrapbook had dozens of sample backgrounds—I could also purchase more selections to add to the software's graphics library. However, keep in mind that we could also include traditionally done scrapbook pages. All you need to do is scan the page and include it in your digital scrapbook file as a photo. This software also has some special effects that includes shadowing photos, framing photos, and selecting shape cutouts that allow a photo to take the shape of a star or flower.

5 Open the scrapbook. This software includes the option of having a set of thumbnails (top), and table of contents (bottom). You can keep these options or just delete the pages.

You can create a color background for a page or select a theme. Under Options you'll find the screen box that lets you select page background by color or theme. If you select color, you will be shown a color palette.

6 Flip to the first page with a photo.

Here's an example of simple, single color.

Then you'll be able to paste your image onto the paper.

Another option is a decorative background.

You can select cropping templates.

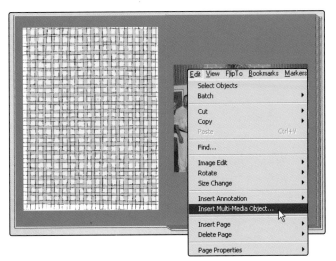

You can import your own background papers onto the pages. It's called Inserting a Multi-Media Object.

You can choose a frame, and select a color for it.

This program refers to using text as an annotation. You have lots of options including selection of font, size, and color. You do the journaling in translucent mode, which puts it in a colored box.

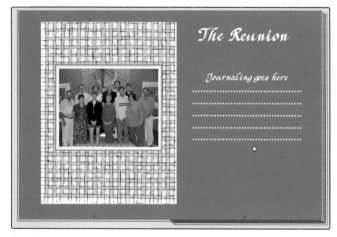

Or, the box can be transparent so it appears as if the journaling was hand lettered onto the page.

SOUND SENSATIONS

Sound and music are as vital to our memories as photos and other memorabilia. I've included sound in this book because I know how wonderful it is to hear a family member's voice and how valuable that voice clip will become over time to future generations. Of course, we have camcorders and digital video recorders that capture not just sound but visuals as well. However, there is something very moving about hearing a clear, strong voice speaking from the past without visual distraction.

Adding Sound

Incorporating sound elements into your digital scrapbooks or electronic slide shows means you insert sound as part of the digital whole. However, it shouldn't be the only time you incorporate sound into your scrapbooking. You can add a pocket to a page and slide in a musical CD, or place a decorated jewel box onto the front of an album, or make it part of the last page of a scrapbook. And, as a side note from one scrapbooker to another, even if digital isn't the way you want to go, please consider making an audiotape to include with a scrapbook.

There are several ways to incorporate sound into your scrapbook elements—you can record a voice with a computer microphone, use music bits from your audio tapes/CDs, or download files from the Web.

The two most popular audio or music file formats are WAV and MP3. WAV files is the format used by the audio CDs you purchase. This format is similar to TIFF picture files because a WAV file is not compressed. It is a raw digital file, and this means a big file that uses lots of memory. For example, it can take 20 Mbytes of memory for a three-minute song.

MP3 files are similar in function to JPEGs. This file compresses the music to a much smaller format that takes less memory and is faster to download. By comparison, an MP3 file only takes one to two Mbytes for a three-minute song and is almost indistinguishable from a WAV file. Both formats are in wide use, and are supported by common computer audio/media players.

To embed or include a WAV or MP3 file into a traditional scrapbook, you will record the sound and copy it onto a diskette or CD (see page 28). You can create any variety of pockets on your pages to hold the CD or diskette (see page 145). In order to hear the sound, a computer needs to have software installed, such as Media Player, to play the sound from the diskette or CD.

You can add sound to a digital scrapbook or slide show by simply inserting the sound as the software program instructs. In most digital scrapbook and slide show software packages, the ability to hear the sound (on anyone's computer) is included as a feature of the software.

COPYRIGHTED MUSIC

Please use your common sense in following the law when it comes to including sound in your scrapbooking efforts. Just as you must keep copyright laws in mind when scrapbooking—you can't personally copy professional photographs or scan and print copyrighted decorative paper—you must be aware that most copyright laws protect mainstream music.

There is also much debate about whether downloading music from the web without paying for its use is legal. It is also considered a violation to give a family member or friend music you have purchased but copied onto cassette tapes, CDs, or as an MP3. Unlike computer software programs where it is considered okay to make a backup copy, the music industry doesn't give you this right when you purchase an album or single.

RECORDING A SOUND BITE

Since most recording software records only short amounts of sound at a time—usually up to a minute—it's essential to first prepare and practice what you want to say.

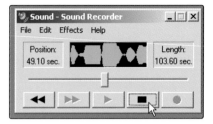

1 When you feel confident, turn on the microphone and open the software. Click the record button (shown as the red dot). Speak, sing, or laugh!

2 When done, click on the stop button (shown as the black rectangle). Play back the recording. You can re-record if necessary. Once you've got the recording you want you can click the File button, then Save. Type in a name for the file, then save.

3 To play the sound, all you need to do is open the file by clicking on it, and your software for sound will open and play the WAV file.

DIGITAL SLIDE SHOW

When you have a large group of photos you want to share, such as photos from a vacation or wedding, presenting them to friends and family in a digital slide-show format rather than as digital scrapbook pages is best.

Some digital scrapbooking software includes a slide show feature, where, with just the click of a button, your digital scrapbook becomes a slide show. However, this isn't always the best way to get the feel of a slide show. A digital scrapbook works best when journaling is present. After all it's the journaling that tells the story behind the photos.

A slide show should let the photos do the talking. Most digital scrapbooking software will only create a slide show of photos or images. Your journaling, including titles and captions, usually isn't included.

For creating my slide shows, I prefer using PowerPoint. Though it was really designed for business applications, it's easily adapted for more personal presentations. Other slide show software includes Digital Photo Slide Show, PictureShow, ShowMaker, and MySlideShow. I find that Power-Point allows for the most creativity and ease of use, but all programs share the basic features in the slide show format. Unlike most digital scrap-books, slide show programs don't offer much in the way of photo editing. You'll want to do your entire photo editing before you start, and save the digital images in a single folder. Then you can insert the folder into your slide show program.

GETTING STARTED WITH HELP AND OPTIONS

You'll have three choices when you create this kind of slide show.

The first is AutoContent Wizard. The wizard is a tutorial that uses detailed explanations that take you step by step to a complete slide show. This is a slow process, but for a beginner who has very little background in computers, this may be the best option.

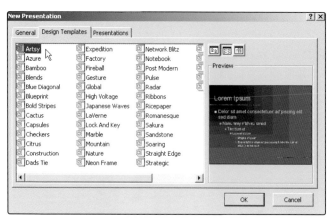

The second option is called Design Template, which means there is a predefined background applied to all slides you create. You also have the option of creating your own design with Blank Presentation. With it, you do not choose preset color themes or background graphics as you would in Design Template.

If you select Design Template, you'll be given a choice of design templates to work from. This is an example of a template design. Your background or theme is set for all your slides.

CREATING THE SLIDE SHOW

Open the software. Decide if you want to use a template or blank. Most beginners feel more comfortable using a template, which lays out a specific graphic with predetermined title and text, but brazen creative types usually opt for blank presentation. Let's go for it and select blank presentation.

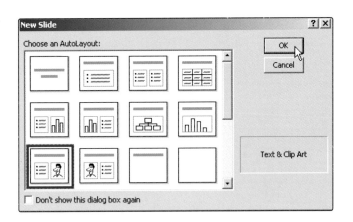

A selection of choices will appear for your first slide. The selections predefine automatic locations for text and picture on all slides. You'll fill in the information for titles, text, or graphics.

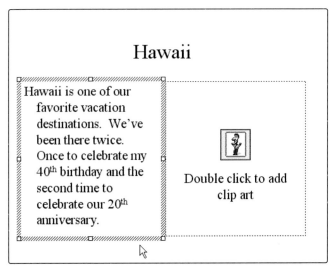

2 My first slide selection will be a slide that has a title, text, and photo area layout. We'll select the template that includes all three. Type in the title and your text (journaling). Double click on the clip art/graphic box. Select to import clip or graphic.

3 This opens a browser so you can find the photo you want to insert. Find and select photo.

Hawaii

Hawaii is one of our favorite vacation destinations. We've been there twice. Once to celebrate my 40th birthday and the second time to celebrate our 20th anniversary.

4 This is the first finished slide. Save your slide, and click on New Slide (under Insert in toolbar). After your first slide is prepared and saved, every New Slide will give you a choice of template layout.

Water everywhere... rivers, ponds, waterfalls, and ocean

5 For slide 2, I selected a blank slide with no predetermined layout, so I could insert a photo and some journaling.

November 2, 2000 Molokai, Hawaii

6 For slide three, I used only one photo, but enlarged the graphics box to make the photo larger.

7 For slide four, I added three graphics boxes and imported three photos.

Fun and Creative Features

There is a variety of additional creative elements you can add to your slide show. You can customize the way the slide is wiped to and from the screen by selecting a Transition. If you don't want fancy or busy wipes to distract from the slide show photographs, then just click No Transition. You can add sound with a selection of sound effects provided by the software package, or you can pull up your own sound bytes, WAVs, or MP3s.

You can also add animation to your slide show in this program. You can have a title pop or explode onto the slide. Animation is fun when used in small quantities. Too much animation distracts from the photos and text.

Just like a traditional scrapbook, you can opt to include text like dates, locations, and other tidbits. All you need to do is go to the toolbar feature Insert. Click to insert an additional text box. Size the text box to coordinate with your slide (meaning you might want it large or maybe just small text in the right-hand corner). Another way to add all your dates, locations, places, and names is to have an intro slide or an ending/indexing slide.

To preview the slide show, just click on the Slide Show button, and click on View Slide Show. Make any changes you wish, and then save the slide show under the File button.

Capturing the Emotion of Motion

You can add some spice to your digital scrapbooking skills by including small movies called AVI or MPEG files. These files can be added to digital scrapbooks and in some slide show programs. You can also burn these clips to a CD. AVI and MPEG are to video what JPEG is to graphics and the MP3 is to sound. They are small compressed files that don't take up much room or memory.

You can create AVIs or MPEGs from videotapes with a connector plug that will connect your video camera to the computer. You'll need video-editing software too, unless you are a brilliant director and a one-take wonder.

However, there is an easier way to get a mini movie. You can use your digital camera! Most digital cameras include a feature that allows for a brief video that lasts for up to 40 seconds. Once you've recorded this video, you can transfer it into your computer the same way you transfer any digital image/photo from the camera-either by a cable connection or a card reader.

Most video files will need a media player. There are many options for this type of software, and you should select the software program that best fits your preferences or needs. Media players like Windows Media Player or RealOne Player will play sound, music, and video. The players let you both record and play. Keep in mind that many media players will want to be your main player and have file formats that aren't compatible with other media players. Look for programs that record or play more universally accepted formats like AVI (video), MPEG (video), WAV (music), and MP3 (music).

Software like MusicMatch Jukebox, Audio MP3 Converter, and AudioUtilities will convert audio files from one format to another like an MP3 to a WAV or a WMA to an MP3.

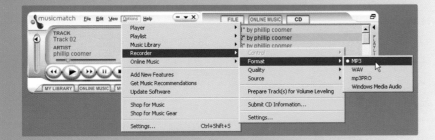

1. Open software. Insert an audio CD into the CD drive.

2. Select tracks or songs that you want to convert. Click Copy. This example shows the conversion to MP3 file.

3. Songs are now copied as MP3s and will be placed into My Music folder or folder of your choice. You can now use the MP3 files on most digital features from mail lists, e-mail, scrapbooks, and slide shows.

To be aboveboard and worry free with copyright laws, you should only add copyright- and royalty-free music to anything you create. You can purchase copyright- and royalty-free music on the Internet or by mail order.

London Page

Away from home? Share the experience by sending a memorable digital page to friends and family. The page can become part of a digital scrapbook, or can be printed out for a traditional scrapbook.

MATERIALS

Photographs

Ephemera, such as bus passes, postcards, and brochures

SOFTWARE & TOOLS

Flatbed Scanner with scanning software

Adobe PhotoShop software

Designer: Shannon Yokeley

INSTRUCTIONS

1. Assemble the items on the scanner and preview the image. Continue rearranging and previewing the image until you are happy. Scan the image at 300 dpi and 100 percent.

2. Once you have the image in the photo-editing program, adjust the color and sharpen if necessary.

3. Save the image as a TIFF if you are going to print it out, or as a JPEG for sending digitally.

It's a Dog's Life

Including a CD in your scrapbook pages means devising a pocket for holding it. On first glance, this looks like a whimsical page using traditional skills to show off a furry family member. But tucked behind the photo is a pocket that holds the CD with a digital slide show of (what else?) the dog's life.

Designer: Maria Nerius

MATERIALS

4 sheets of coordinating, decorative, acid-free paper
Photo
Mesh paper
Blank CD
CD label

SOFTWARE & TOOLS

Acid-free adhesive
Scanner
Printer
Photo-editing software
Scissors or paper trimmer
Word-processing/journaling software
Paper glue
Labeling software

INSTRUCTIONS

1. To make the pocket, first fold one of your decorative sheets in half with the right side facing out. Apply a very thin line of glue along each of the side edges. Firmly press the sides for a tight bond. Set aside to dry.

2. If necessary, scan the photo and crop, then resize to approximately 7 x 4½ inches (17.5 x 11.3 cm). Mat the photo on decorative paper. Then mat onto the pocket paper.

3. Using your word-processing/journaling software, create a title with a caption. Print and trim.

4. Using glue, adhere the pocket to the bottom half of your background paper.

5. Cut the mesh paper to approximately 8 x 5¼ inches (20.3 x 13.3cm), and position it on the top half of the background paper. Trim the decorative paper that will be over the mesh paper to a size that, when centered, will leave a 1-inch (2.5 cm) border of mesh showing. Place glue on the back of the decorative paper and adhere to the mesh paper. Adhere title and caption.

6. Create the CD. Create the CD label using labeling software.

Margaret Is Growing Up

This whimsical time line makes good use of digital and conventional snapshots. As you can see, cropping photos is not limited to boxes. You can create special effects by silhouetting, which allows you to crop a person or element in a photo and place it where you want it.

MATERIALS

Textured item in a solid color
Photos
Rubber stamp

SOFTWARE & TOOLS

Scanner
Photo-editing software
Desktop publishing software, or
   Word-processing software

Note: This project is more advanced for those who work with desktop publishing programs. You can get similar, though not exact, results with your word-processing program using the Draw features.

Margaret Rose is growing up!

Born on April 4, 1998 in Atlanta, Georgia, she arrived on a very blustery day.

Margaret was walking at 9 months, and running on her 1st birthday.

Sunflower from the Atlanta garden, the summer before Margaret was born.

Designer: Susan McBride

INSTRUCTIONS

1. For the textured background, scan an item that will give you the texture you seek. A linen napkin was used for this page. Scan in any other images you need. The bee on this page is a scanned rubber stamp. You can also scan in clip art images.

She spends a lot of time outdoors, in the garden or hiking in the mountains with her mom, dad and dog, Luna.

Margaret is a curious child, she wants to know about everything.

Wearing the butterfly dress from Grandma Dolly at the Botanical Garden in Asheville.

in that program that isolates an image. First you use a drawing tool to outline your object to isolate it, then you save it as a JPEG or TIFF file. You can then import it into the program you are working with. Many photo-editing programs provide similar ways to silhouette.

4. Note that two photos appear in circles. There are two ways to do this. You can crop the photo into a circle using the circular cropping tool in the photo-editing software, as was done for the circle photo at the right. Or you can import your photo into a circle that you created on your page. The wide white border around the baby's picture to the left was placed around a circle made on the page, then the photo was imported in to it.

5. Assemble your page. Begin by importing the background, then place your photos, and add text. The dotted beeline is easily made using your Draw feature to draw the line then converting it to round dots in the thickness you want.

2. The photos on these pages are a combination of digital photos and scanned snapshots. Save both digital and scanned photos as either JPEGs or TIFF files then import them into your desktop publishing or word-processing program.

3. The designer used PhotoShop to create the silhouettes of the little girl and flower using Creating Paths, which is an option provided

6. You can keep these pages as all-digital, placing them in a digital scrapbook or sending them out via the internet. Or, you can print them out for your traditional scrapbook.

CD Labels and Jackets

Once you put your digital scrapbook pages on CDs, it's easy to personalize them and the jewel box cases by creating your own labels. Even without words, the pictures easily identify the content and serve as an introduction to the presentation.

MATERIALS
Photos
Labels

SOFTWARE & TOOLS
Labeling software
Printer
Label stomper

Designer: Maria Nerius

INSTRUCTIONS

1. Open your label software. Select whether to make from scratch or to use a template. If you will be using a template, you will just add text into the given text boxes and then print. If you will be creating from scratch, continue with the following instructions.

2. Select and import the photo or graphic. Use the cursor to size the image up or down to make it fit on the label.

3. Add any text boxes by clicking on the Text command or feature, then add text.

4. Make any adjustments for balance and design, and save the label.

5. Place the CD label sheet into your printer. Note if you have a top- or bottom-feed printer, and adjust accordingly. Print the label.

6. If you use a stomper to apply the label to the CD, follow the manufacturer's instructions. In most cases, you will remove the paper backing from the label and place the label onto the stomper with the adhesive side up. Place the CD on the stomper with the right side down. Press the stomper to adhere the label to the CD, then remove the labeled CD from the stomper.

Note: There are two kinds of CD labels. One has a large center hole, and the other has a smaller hole that matches the small hole in the CD. If you want to use photographs, you'll get the best results from the label with the smaller hole. Labels also come in different papers like glossy and matte. Glossy label paper is best for photos.

Jackets

Most CD label software has a feature for creating CD jackets. The materials and tools are the same for making the CD labels.

1. Open your label software. Select whether to make from scratch or use a template. If you will be using a template, you will just add text into the given text boxes and then print. If you will be creating from scratch, continue with the instructions.

2. Select and import the photo or graphic. Use the cursor to size the image up or down to fit on the jacket. Jacket labels can come in one or two parts—just for the front, or for the front and back. If you are working with two parts, you will design each one separately.

3. Add any text boxes by clicking on the Text command or feature, then add text.

4. Make any adjustments for balance and design, and save the jacket.

5. Place the jacket sheet into your printer. Note if you have a top- or bottom-feed printer, and adjust accordingly. Print the jacket. Insert the printed jacket into the CD jewel box.

Designer: Maria Nerius

Acknowledgments

I would like to thank the following companies whose products I've enjoyed using over the years and that I used within this book: Randy Benson, pcCrafters Software, Sony, Mendy Werne, E-Books, Visual Horizons, Hot Off The Press, Creating Keepsakes, Epson, Arnold Grummer's, Hewlett Packard, Kodak, Fuji, DMD Industries Paper Reflections, Saral Paper, Fiskars, Therm O Web, and McGill Inc. More information about these companies can be found on the Lark Books website.

Thanks to everyone at Lark Books especially my editor, Jane LaFerla, who put in many long hours. Her skill with words, organization, and grammar made this a book I can be proud of. This book was a true team effort. I'd also like to thank the art director, Celia Naranjo, Lark Books' Vice-President and Publishing Director Carol Taylor, and Executive Assistant to the Publishing Director Nicole Tuggle. Special thanks to designers Terry Taylor, Shannon Yokeley, and Susan McBride for creating additional pages for this book.

A round of applause and sincere appreciation for the help (technical and otherwise) of Steve Summers, Jim Given, Bill Gardner, and Phillip Coomer.

I couldn't have completed this book without my wonderful family and friends who shared laughs, love, memories and many photographs. Many thanks to Elizabeth and Clem Conklin, Jeff Nerius, Ingrid Ginther and her girls, Brenda Given, Ron Given, Bill Given, Jeff Given, Aunt Wanda, Uncle Ron, Terryl Given, Mary Jo, Tollee, Vivian Summers, Marilyn and Mel Russell, Stephanie Friday, Nancee McAteer, Dr. Thomas Priest and his wonderful staff, Max, Moe, Sam, Claude Byrum and Helena. And finally to that handsome electrical engineering major who was my childhood sweetheart and is now the most wonderful husband in the world. I want to thank Ken Nerius for all his technical expertise, honest feedback, and all the time he spent reviewing my drafts when he could have been playing volleyball.

Index